It's a God Thing

ONE WOMAN EXPERIENCES SIGNS, MIRACLES, AND WONDERS, TRUSTING GOD

LEISA SPANN

Chasing Kites
publishing

It's a God Thing: One Woman Experiences Signs, Miracles, and Wonders, Trusting God.

LEISA SPANN
2637 ROUNDHILL ROAD
OAK GROVE, LA. 71263

Website: LEISASPANN.COM
Email: leisaspann@yahoo.com

ISBN (paperback):   978-0-9997356-5-7

Dedication

I dedicate this book to those who are LOST, and don't know JESUS as their Lord and Savior. For those that HUNGER and THIRST for more, there is more!
Jesus replied,

> **"I am the bread of life. Whoever comes to Me will never be hungry again. Whoever believes in Me will never be thirsty." John 6:35 | NLT**

No matter who you are, or what you've done,
no matter what others think of you,
or what you think of yourself!
The lonely are loved, the hurting are healed,
the guilty are forgiven,
and the lost are found!

YOU ARE HIS, AND YOU ARE LOVED!!!

Contents

CONTENTS

Prologue

Have you ever wondered if God really speaks to people the way He did with Moses and others in the Bible? Can God orchestrate signs, miracles, and wonders today? There are so many people that say and try to prove there is no God.

God came first, the Bible says:

> *In the beginning God created the heavens and the earth. Genesis 1:1 | NLT*

I would rather believe God was here first and created the universe than believe the universe was here already. If God is not real, then neither is Jesus. I can't make you believe in Jesus. That comes only by faith. But maybe by the time you finish reading my true experiences of times I trusted God with all my heart in every aspect of my life, receiving signs, miracles, and wonders, you will also believe. I'm thankful that God always uses at least one other person to verify the miraculous in my own life.

I want you all to know about the miraculous signs and wonders the Most High God has performed for me. How great are His signs; how powerful His wonders! His kingdom will last forever, His rule through all generations. Daniel 4:2-3 | NLT

For those who are lost, after reading, I pray you will believe God is real, and God sent His son, Jesus, to save this world.

For those who once believed, maybe you lost your way. When you read about how God saved me twice within a couple of months and spared me from the depths of HELL, I pray you will find your way back and your strength and joy will be restored.

For those who already believe, I pray your FAITH will soar.

In my younger years, I did not like school. I quit at the beginning of my eleventh-grade year. Math and English were my worst subjects, and PE was my favorite. Never in a million years would I have thought to write poetry, much less a book. However, when I was thirty-five years old, I re-dedicated my life to Jesus, and my life changed. That's when I found out, *"WITH GOD ALL THINGS ARE POSSIBLE."* (Matthew 19:26)

In February 2000, I was invited to go to another church where Evangelist Brother Names would be speaking. I really didn't want to go, especially after working all day, standing on my feet. However, God told me to go, so I decided I would since it was important to Him.

That night was the first night I experienced the power of God! I was called to the front, scared to death and wondering what in the world this man of God was going to tell me.

Now, I would have to say I was a skeptic. That's when Brother Names looked at me and said, *"You really love angels, don't you?"*

Well, my thought at that time was, *Yeah, every woman and me in here!* However, I replied, *"Yes."*

Then he said, *"And you love writing about them, too. And when God gives you the words, they start flowing."* Well, that definitely hit a nerve! My eyes started to water, and my knees started to shake. I knew this man was in touch with God, and God was telling him what to say.

In 1999, I started writing poetry, and the first poems I wrote (other than the one about my Papaw) were titled: *"An Angel is a Sister," "An Angel is a Mother,"* and *"An Angel is a Friend."*

Brother Names even told what my guardian angel's name was.

For He will order His angels to protect you wherever you go. Psalms 91:11 | NLT

He also said, *"You will see an angel one day, and it will appear in your vehicle."*

My thought was, *I hope my vehicle is sitting still when this happens.* Ha!

Finally, he walked up to me with his pointer finger and barely touched my forehead. It was as if I was as light as a feather. When Brother Names did this, I fell straight back and hit the floor, waking up with my head halfway under the pew, thinking, *How did I get this way? I feel as if God just breathed on me!*

Maybe this was why God wanted me to go, so I could feel the Power of the Holy Spirit. What I felt even more though was the power of His love.

Before this experience, I would ask God every now and then if it was all real? Not that it would make any difference if I never knew, as far as being committed to God. I wanted everything God had for me, and I wanted to know all about who God was!

After the service, I walked up to Brother Names to thank him, and as I was shaking his hand, he tilted his head a bit as if God was giving him words again. He looked at me and said, *"I want to read your book!"* I laughed and thought, *Well now he has me confused with someone else! Writing poetry was one thing, but a book is a much bigger thing!*

After a long, eighteen-year journey, that prophecy has come to pass. Now you know how this book came to be. As you read, you will see how God used me and how I received signs, miracles, and wonders.

God speaks to us all, are you listening?

Anyone with ears to hear should listen and understand! Matthew 11:15 | NLT

CHAPTER 1

God Spoke My Name

One day, while on the phone with my mom, she told me about an experience she had when she was five months pregnant with me. Mom said, *"I was having trouble with my pregnancy, and your Aunt Rachel talked me into going to the revival with her."*

I knew my Aunt Rachel was Pentecostal, and my mom was Baptist. My mom had also never been to a Pentecostal Church before. I knew this story was about to get very interesting. I am Pentecostal too, and my mom made comments to me about how we jump the pews and swing from the rafters. (Just for the record, we do not do that.)

She continued with the story, *"When we got to the revival, your Aunt Rachel told the congregation that I was having trouble, so they put me in a chair at the front of the church and started doing a war dance around me. I got so upset with what they were doing, they had to take me to the hospital."*

At that very moment, I burst out laughing at the image of the *"war dance."* I could visualize all the ladies there praying for me as they circled around my mom on my behalf—that God would save the pregnancy and I would live. That's when I heard God say, *"Leisa, I spoke your name before you were ever born!"* At that very moment, I realized I do have a purpose.

For I know the plans I have for you, says the Lord. They are plans for good and not for disaster, to give you a future and a hope. In those days when you pray, I will listen. If you look for Me wholeheartedly, you will find Me. Jeremiah 29:11-13 | NLT

Have you ever wondered why you were born? Why did God want you here and what is your purpose? Why do you have to go through trials and tribulations in life? Why do some of us feel at times unworthy, unloved, or like we are the black sheep of the family?

That's a lot of WHY's, and I have asked myself each one at different times. Perhaps you have as well.

Do we ever find our purpose? How do we know when we've found it? Did we search hard enough? Maybe our searching should be as intent as a child searching for the prized Easter Egg. You know the saying, *"Look under every nook and cranny."*

Now seek the Lord your God with all your heart and soul. 1 Chronicles 22:19 | NLT

Did we already fill our purpose in life and not know it? Maybe if we knew how important our role is to God, we would care more about what our purpose is. One's specific purpose is not greater than another. To God, they are all equal because He loves us all the same. However, God will sometimes choose someone specific for a larger assignment because He knows they are the only one that can do it, like Noah. He got the job done and didn't care that people said he was crazy; he didn't care that they laughed. He knew what his purpose was and accomplished it.

It was by faith that Noah built a large boat to save his family from the flood. He obeyed God, who warned him about things that had never happened before. By his faith, Noah condemned the rest of the world, and he received the righteousness that comes by faith. Hebrews 11:7 | NLT

Maybe your purpose was to befriend someone because you would love them for who they are and would encourage them to find their purpose in life. Or maybe your purpose was to save someone's life in a car accident. You were meant to be there at that very second, and you were the only one that could do it. So do you think saving the person's life who was in the car accident is greater than befriending someone? NO! Why? Because maybe the person who God sent to befriend another would eventually write a book that would save souls and be a light in a dark world.

"The two most important days in your life are the day you were born and the day you find out why." Mark Twain

Maybe you are still looking, or maybe you have already filled your purpose in life. It's hard to believe God can orchestrate all of our lives that way, but He can and He does.

We know that God causes everything to work together for the good of those who love God and are called according to His purpose for them.
Romans 8:28 | NLT

I can tell you God knew your name before you were born and gave you a purpose.

But even before I was born, God chose me and called me by His marvelous grace.
Galatians 1:15 | NLT

You made all the delicate, inner parts of my body and knit me together in my mother's womb. Thank You for making me so wonderfully complex! Your workmanship is marvelous—how well I know it. You watched me as I was being formed in utter seclusion, as I was woven together in the dark of the womb. You saw me before I was born. Every day of my life was recorded in Your book. Every moment was laid out before a single day had passed.
Psalms 139:13-16 | NLT

CHAPTER 2

Finding My Purpose

When I was fifteen years old, I accepted Jesus as my Lord and Savior.

> *For God loved the world so much that He gave His one and only Son so that everyone who believes in Him will not perish but have eternal life. John 3:16 | NLT*

However, being a Christian teen in school wasn't *"cool."* I eventually lost my way as a Christian because I wanted to be popular. Ironically, I didn't receive the popularity I wanted, and I lost my relationship with Jesus as well.

Sometimes we do get lost or backslide. At times we should have turned one way rather than another. However, God never gives up on us. Our purpose is still there! Just like a GPS system, He recalculates a route for us when we take a detour from the one intended. It may take longer to arrive at our destination, but if it's our desire to seek Him and do His will, He will show himself to us in a mighty way.

I took a lot of wrong turns before I decided to seek God.

A few years passed since that time in high school. I married young and had a daughter, Nicole, soon after. My mother-in-law, Wilhelmina, was a praying, God-fearing woman. She called me every Saturday evening to ask, *"Would you and Nicole like to go to church with me in the morning?"*

My reply each time was, *"Mrs. Wilhelmina, I don't like the church you go to!"* However, she never gave up on me. She continued to call me every Saturday evening for months.

One Saturday, I decided I had enough. When she called that evening, I answered the phone and stated, *"Mrs. Wilhelmina, I will go to church with you in the morning just this once so you will leave me alone. Don't ask me again because I will not go!"*

Since her church was Pentecostal, I was uneasy and terrified of what might happen. I had no idea what to expect. However, what did happen was something I'd never experienced. The young pastor's name was Brother Bill, and as he preached, he ran, skipped, and sometimes danced. He was constantly moving from one side to the other, never staying behind the pulpit. It was as if he had ants in his pants and was on fire; he couldn't be still.

He preached with such authority and passion, and I had never heard preaching like this. With every move he made, my eyes followed. My ears were burning for more of God's Word. I was afraid to look away, thinking that I would miss something. Not once did I look at my watch to see the time. I didn't want the service to end, and it left me wanting more. I was still afraid of the unknown. Yet, it captivated me enough that I went back the next Sunday. Every time I went to church, I left wanting more.

A couple of years later, I found myself divorced. Once again, I backslid and Jesus was out of my life. Even though I was no longer married to Mrs. Wilhelmina's son, I knew she continued to pray for me daily. I knew God would never give up on me, but because of my wrongs, there were times I felt He would. When in reality, I was the one who moved away from Him.

I soon found a job at Walmart, so Nicole and I started living in an apartment within the city limits of Oak Grove, Louisiana. One particular night, Nicole stayed at my mom's house since my shift was from 3:00 to 9:00 p.m. After work, when I arrived at my apartment, I decided to cook some rice. When it started to boil, I decided I didn't want it anymore, so I grabbed the pot and poured it down my garbage disposal.

I obviously wasn't thinking because a few minutes later I noticed the sink was clogged from the rice, as it had continued to swell.

I was there by myself with no idea what to do. I got down on the floor, opened the cabinet doors under the sink, and just sat there, staring at the pipes as if I could possibly do something. Sulking in disgust over what I had just done and feeling stupid for pouring the rice down the sink, I suddenly felt pressure on top of my right shoulder. It was as if someone was standing behind me and had placed their hand on me.

At that very second, fear came over me. My heart started pounding rapidly as if I was going to burst. I was supposed to be home alone. I turned around quickly and saw no one. *How is that possible?* I thought to myself. I knew what I had felt. I sat there, still shaking from what had just happened, when suddenly tears started to stream down my face. As I processed what just happened, I felt it had been Jesus who had stood behind me, that He had placed His hand on my shoulder as a gesture. He was still with me.

Do not be afraid or discouraged, for the Lord will personally go ahead of you. He will be with you; He will neither fail you nor abandon you. Deuteronomy 31:8 | NLT

Still, that wasn't enough for me to turn my life around or turn back to Him. A year later, I married my now husband,

Gary, and we had our daughter, Chelsi. I was very happy with my new life but felt empty inside. I had hunger and thirst for the Word of God, and I wanted to go back to my church. However, my husband wasn't Pentecostal and didn't want to go there. He said, *"If we are going to church, it will be with my family."* Once again, I did nothing because I wanted to go to my church, so I didn't go at all.

A few more years went by, and I needed laparoscopic knee surgery. During the week after surgery, my calf began to hurt every time I would walk or flex my foot. When I went for my checkup at the doctor's office, I told my doctor about the pain I was having in my calf. His reply was, *"It's probably just irritation from the surgery. If it doesn't go away in a few days, come back."*

A few days passed, and the pain was gone. I was now having back pain from lying down often, trying to stay off of my feet. I then noticed I had pain in my groin every time I sat down or stood up. I called the chiropractor's office for an appointment to see about my back, and he was able to see me that same day.

I asked him to do the shock treatment on my lower back. After thirty minutes of treatment, my back felt much better, though when I left, the pain in my groin was still there. I had a small back vibration machine at home that I used when I couldn't go to the chiropractor. I decided when I got home I would place it on my groin; maybe that would help. After about five minutes of using the machine, the pain was still there. I thought, *Maybe I pulled a muscle, and it will get better with time.*

Around midnight, I woke up crying in pain. Every time my heart beat, my leg throbbed. When I decided to get up, I noticed my leg was swollen, and the color was distorted.

By this time, my husband was awake and asked, *"Do you want me to take you to the emergency room?"* I replied, *"No, I don't want to get the kids up in the middle of the night. We can go in the morning."*

It was noon the next day before I arrived at the hospital. I took my sweet time getting there even though my leg was a scary sight. I was in the emergency room when I found out I had three blood clots in my leg. One had already moved from the calf of my leg to my groin. I knew this wasn't good, and I could no longer hold back my tears. As I was lying there crying, I started to wonder, *Am I going to live to see tomorrow, my family, and friends again?* I was afraid the death angel would come visit me during the night.

After everything I had done to myself, not knowing, of course, that blood clots could have killed me, God spared me. I was in the hospital for nine days and then had to take medicine to thin my blood for six months. Two months passed when I realized I had a bladder infection. The doctor called in a prescription for antibiotics for me. When I picked them up from the pharmacy, I noticed they were different. I had never taken these antibiotics before.

About thirty minutes after I took my first dose, as I was sitting on my bedroom floor watching TV, my lips suddenly felt like they were on fire, like I had just bitten into the hottest jalapeno pepper ever. I hopped up off of the floor, mentioned it to my husband, and went to the bathroom to look in the mirror where I found that both my face and my lips were swollen. I just kept thinking, What's going on with me?

I told my husband, *"I'm going to call Libby at home."* She was the pharmacist at Walmart where I worked at the time. I explained to her what was going on, and she told me, *"Get off of the phone and go to the emergency room fast. You are having an allergic reaction to your antibiotics."*

Ha, I was totally dumb to the fact that I was knocking at death's back door—again. Even though Libby told me to get to the emergency room quick, I took my time—again. About ten minutes passed, and I noticed that I wasn't able to breathe in enough air, so my husband decided to call 911.

Five minutes later, we heard a knock on the door. Linda, someone I knew who was also an EMT, was at our doorstep. She was in the area when she heard the call over her radio. I had known Linda for a long time, but she didn't know where I lived. When Linda walked in, she had no idea who I was. My face and lips were so badly swollen that she didn't recognize me. Linda knelt down beside me and held my hand. She tried to comfort me by saying, *"The ambulance will be here shortly."*

Linda knew I was experiencing anaphylaxis (a severe allergic reaction) and felt helpless. Yet, she showed no indication that this would turn out bad. I looked at her and asked, *"Am I going to be okay?"*

Linda's reply was, *"You're going to be fine."*

The ambulance finally arrived, and I was rushed to my hometown hospital. I had the oxygen mask on at full force as I desperately tried to breathe. By this time, I started to breathe harder, going into panic mode. Thinking to myself, Is this it, God? Do I even ask for a third chance? In reality, I had plenty of chances to get my life straight and seek God.

While I was still en route to the hospital, I felt that I needed to shut my eyes and try to keep calm. With my eyes still closed, I arrived at the emergency room and chaos swirled everywhere around me. Workers started pulling on my arms trying to get an IV in my veins. They moved from one arm to the other with no success. All I could hear was the chaos.

I wanted to ask what was going on, but I also really didn't want to know. I was breathing in as much oxygen as I could, which didn't feel like very much as it became harder and harder to do so. I felt a sense of calmness and dizziness at the same time. Again I thought, *Is this it?*

Suddenly, I felt the impacted force of a needle pierce through my jeans into the top of my thigh. I had no warning that was coming. With my eyes still closed, I heard a voice say, *"You're going to be okay."*

Ten minutes later, I was able to breathe on my own again and wanted to go home, but they insisted that I stay overnight. Once again, God spared my life, and I wanted to know why. I had two near-death experiences within two months of each other. I knew something was up, and God finally had my attention.

The next morning, I was released from the hospital. I went by Walmart to get my prescription filled when I ran into Linda, the EMT. She stopped me to say, *"I sure am glad to see you are okay."* She then asked, *"Do you remember when you asked me if you were going to be okay?"*

I said, *"Yes."*

She replied, *"I was praying you would be. I really didn't know if you would make it or not."* In that moment, God confirmed what I already knew: once again, I had been near death.

The following Sunday morning, I woke up determined to find out why God had spared my life—twice. I planned to seek Him with all my heart and soul!

But from there you will search again for the Lord
your God. And if you search for Him with all your
heart and soul, you will find Him.
Deuteronomy 4:29 | NLT

I said to my husband, *"I'm going to church this morning,*
and I'm going to my church. You are more than welcome to
come with me. God has something waiting for me, and I'm
going to find out what it is."

I started going back to my church. However, Brother Bill
was no longer there.

The Church had a new pastor. His name was Brother
Geary. Like Brother Bill, he had a fire, authority, and passion
when preaching. Brother Geary was a Louisiana State Officer
before following God's calling to preach. When I heard this,
I thought, *Why in the world would he go from being a State*
Officer to a preacher?

I later found out that when God calls you to do something, you do it. You will live a miserable life if you run from
your purpose.

A few months later I was at church when Brother Geary
finished his sermon and started the Invitation Call. I was sitting toward the back with my head bowed, patiently waiting
for someone to walk to the front and acknowledge Jesus as
their Savior.

*Everyone who acknowledges Me publicly here on
earth, I will also acknowledge before My Father
in heaven. But everyone who denies Me here
on earth, I will also deny before My Father in
heaven. Matthew 10:32-33 | NLT*

Suddenly, I heard a voice say, *"Leisa, walk to the front of
the church and give your testimony about when you were in the
emergency room with your blood clots."*

My eyes start wandering all around a packed church, trying to figure out what the heck was going on. Who was telling
me to do this? I thought, *I know I just didn't tell myself to do
that because I HATE speaking in front of people. It reminds me
of school and having to stand in front of the class to read what
I wrote.* So if it wasn't me, who was it?

I turned and looked at the back door. I was about to get out
of there because I didn't want any part of that. That's when I
heard it again, *"Leisa, DO NOT walk out of this church before
you walk to the front and give your testimony of when you were
in the emergency room with your blood clots."* Whoever was
speaking to me knew I had just turned and looked at the door
with the thought of escaping out the back.

I sat in fear and whispered, *"God, is that you?"* I was not
moving off of the pew until I received that confirmation. I
then whispered, *"God, if that's you, give me a sign."*

As soon as the words left my lips, Brother Geary said, *"There's someone here who has already been to the emergency room twice." Did my ears just hear that right?,* I thought. Wow! God wanted me to give my testimony about my visits to the emergency room. My knees started to tremble. The fear had set in, and God just spoke to me to confirm it was HIM! Now I needed the strength to get up and walk to the front. My legs felt as if they weighed hundreds of pounds, and I couldn't seem to move them.

What was so amazing to me was that God was talking to Brother Geary at the same time he was talking to me, telling him what to say and telling me what to do. I whispered, *"God, my legs are heavy and don't want to move. You need to give me the strength to get up and walk to the front!"*

As soon as the words left my lips, my knees stopped trembling. I stood up and walked to the front. I told Brother Geary, *"God wanted me to give my testimony of when I was in the emergency room."* He handed me the microphone, and I said, *"There's someone here who is supposed to hear my story. I don't know who you are, but God does."*

I gave my testimony and closed with, *"Instead of worrying if I was going to see my family and friends again, I should have been worried about where I would spend eternity. If I had died, I would have gone straight to Hell!"*

I handed the microphone back to Brother Geary and went to my seat. The moment I sat down, a young mother named

Jeani walked to the front and confessed to accepting Jesus as her Lord and Savior.

Wow, Wow, Wow! Did that just happen?

I felt as if my feet weren't touching the ground—a high you can't get from any drug, that's for sure! And I felt that way for months after what had happened and how God used me.

A few weeks later, on a Wednesday night, Jeani came to me with a big hug after the church service had ended. She told me, *"I know your testimony was for me. I have already been to the emergency room twice within just a few months."*

At that moment I thought, *Did God create me for a reason such as this? Nothing is a coincidence or a mistake with God.*

So was this my only purpose in life? If so, I was totally fine with it. However, I felt God wasn't finished with me yet. There was still a lot more to come!

CHAPTER 3

An Unexpected Gift

A few months after the episode at church, I was still running on high levels of Jesus. Like a drug, I wanted more. My husband and I were surprised when our gift was revealed to us. We were having a baby!

> *Children are a gift from the Lord; they are a*
> *reward from Him. Psalms 127:3 | NLT*

This concerned me because of my age. At thirty-five I was considered a high-risk pregnancy. I sort of felt like Sarah in the Bible. Even though I wasn't near her age, having a baby at thirty-five was old to me. My friends at Walmart started picking on me, saying, *"When this child graduates, they will have to push you in a wheelchair to the graduation."* Ha! What I knew deep down inside was that this child was going to be a boy, and God was going to use him in a mighty way at some point in his life. I didn't know then, and I still don't know now, how God will use him.

When I decided to look for a boy's name, God told me to name our son a Biblical name. A few weeks passed, and I decided to search for the name God intended for him to have. Looking through the Bible at boy names, I decided his name would be Seth.

A week later, however, I knew that wasn't the right name. I pulled out my Bible again to look for names, this time I prayed before I opened it. I asked God to reveal to me the name He intended this child to have. I laid open the Bible and looked down on the page. It was as if all the words were blurred out except for one, which was big and bold. I couldn't miss it: Canaan.

Wow, I thought. That's not a boy's name. That's Canaan, as in *"the promised land."*

Even though it wasn't a boy's name, I knew that's what God wanted me to name him. My husband, Gary, didn't agree with me on this, which we all know is a normal disagreement between spouses. I told him this was going to be our child's name because I knew this was what God wanted. As weeks passed, my husband said, *"The name is growing on me."*

My pregnancy was going well with no problems until my eighth month. I gained a lot of weight and had major swelling. My doctor told me I had to take my leave from work and stay off of my feet. One particular morning, I woke up with a dread that something would be wrong with our child. I only had a few weeks left before the c-section. I didn't know why I had these feelings, and worry began to set in. I couldn't understand why God would allow this to happen. I decided, maybe God was telling me this so I would pray for Canaan before he arrived.

Just as my Mom had done during her pregnancy with me, I decided to go to Walmart so my friends could pray for me and my concerns. As I entered the store, I saw Carol. She was another praying, God-fearing woman!

Before I continue with my story, you must first know who Carol is and why she plays an important part. I went to Carol a few months earlier when God was telling me to tithe my paycheck. I didn't know anything about tithing at that point, and I knew Carol would. One day at work, I stopped her and said, *"Carol, can you tell me more about tithing and how it works?"*

Carol replied, *"Leisa, the Bible says we are to tithe ten percent of our earnings to our church to help in God's Kingdom."*

"Carol, we live paycheck to paycheck, I can't afford to give ten percent," I said.

Carol then said, *"Leisa, I cannot tell you how it works. It just does. You cannot outgive God, and you cannot work it* out on paper either. All I can say is trust God, tithe your ten percent, and God will provide."

Carol continued, "I'll tell you what you can do. Test God. Give your ten percent out of your paycheck, and if you can't pay your bills with what you have left over, stop tithing."

I started tithing my paycheck the following Sunday, and since that day, I've never skipped a beat. My husband and I have been tithing for over twenty years. God has been faithful to us as we have put our trust in Him.

> **Bring all the tithes into the storehouse so there will be enough food in My Temple. "If you do," says the Lord of Heaven's Armies, "I will open the windows of heaven for you. I will pour out a blessing so great you won't have enough room to take it in! Try it! Put Me to the test!"**
> **Malachi 3:10 | NLT**

Now you know why when I saw Carol, I thought, *IT'S A GOD THING for sure!*

When Carol saw me, she stopped me. She could tell something was wrong when she saw the fear on my face. Then another coworker, Jackie, walked up and I told both of them that I feared something was going to be wrong with Canaan. We all held hands right there in the middle of Walmart and started praying.

*If two of you agree here on earth concerning
anything you ask, My Father in heaven will do it
for you. For where two or three gather together as
My followers, I am there among them.
Matthew 18:19-20 | NLT*

I am not ashamed of my relationship with the Lord, and I
do not care what people say or think about me! You have to
be bold as a lion and stand strong in your Faith. Maybe that's
why God has used me like He has over the years.

The time came and off to the hospital we went the evening
before our son's birth, which—August 28. I checked into the
hospital, and they started preparing me for the next morning.
I was trying not to worry or let anyone know how consumed
with fear I really was.

The morning finally arrived and was not off to a very good
start. The pediatrician was over thirty minutes late when she
finally arrived.

But things smoothed out and at last he was born, beautiful with an olive complexion and a head full of black hair. I
asked, *"Is he okay?"* They replied, *"Yes."*

Hours later, when I woke up, the pediatrician came to our
room to tell us our son had been born with Pectus Excavatum,
a congenital deformity of the anterior thoracic wall in which
the sternum and rib cage grow abnormally, which produces a
caved-in or sunken appearance of the chest.

I had tears rolling down my cheeks, trying to hold it all in. I asked them to bring him to me, and they said, *"He has a small problem breathing right now. It's nothing to be concerned about. He will be okay. We just need to watch him."* They finally brought him in to see us for a little while. Understandably, my concern at this point was growing by the hour.

The next morning, which was Friday, I *needed* to see him. To prevent soreness from my c-section, I decided to walk to the nursery. During the day, the nurses would bring him in twice to see us, but only for a total of thirty minutes. I knew something just wasn't right. However, the doctor assured me that Canaan was okay. He just needed a little extra time to get his breathing pattern right.

Saturday morning, my gynecologist came in saying, *"I'm releasing you today."* I asked, *"What about my baby?"*

He said, *"I've talked to the hospital and they are going to give y'all a complimentary room. I believe they are going to release the baby in the morning."*

Sunday morning arrived, and I was preparing to go home with our baby, until one of the nurses came in and said, *"Mr. and Mrs. Spann, I've overstepped my bounds this morning. I called the pediatrician and told her there was something seriously wrong with your son. She is on her way up here to run a few tests."* She started to apologize and said, *"I'm sorry, I couldn't let y'all leave with your son and have something happen to him after you get home."*

A few hours later, the pediatrician came into the room and informed us that our son had pneumothorax, a collection of air in the pleural space, which leads to a collapsed lung. Due to the pressure needed to expand the lungs, a healthy infant can develop an air leak when it takes its first breaths after birth. Such forced pressure causes the lung to collapse. Severe shortness of breath and dangerously low blood pressure are known side effects. If untreated for a prolonged amount of time, a tension pneumothorax can be deadly.

At this point, I totally lost it and burst into tears of agony. I didn't understand anything the pediatrician told us, but I knew it wasn't good. I told my husband to please call his sister, Debbie. She was an RN and could tell us in plain English, not medical talk, what it all meant.

I was falling apart, wondering if my Faith was not enough? I did not dare ask God the big word or question, *"Why?"*

It was Sunday morning, and I called Brother Geary (my pastor). I informed him that Canaan had three days of respiratory distress problems and asked him to please ask the congregation to pray for him. I knew I needed to go pray myself, and I didn't want to pray in my room. I wanted to walk to the chapel, get on my knees to pray, and seek God in prayer. By this time, my sister-in-law, Debbie, had arrived at the hospital and asked if she could go with me to the chapel. I replied, *"Yes."* I knew she was going just in case I totally fell apart while I was there.

*But in my distress I cried out to the Lord; yes, I
prayed to my God for help.
He heard me from His sanctuary; my cry to Him
reached His ears.*
Psalms 18:6 | NLT

I had been in the chapel praying for about fifteen minutes
when I felt a calmness and peace come over me. All my fear
was gone, and I felt Canaan was going to be fine. I got up,
looked at my sister-in-law, and said, *"He's going to be okay!"*
I didn't know how he was going to be okay. I just knew God
was going to intervene.

A couple hours later, we were informed that the NICU
from another hospital was coming for Canaan. They brought
him to my room in an incubator so I could say my goodbyes.
I wanted to fall apart knowing I was going home without
him, but I knew I would see him soon.

That afternoon, our home phone rang. It was a nurse from
the NICU, which was where Canaan was. All the babies in the
NICU have their own nurses, and this particular nurse called
me needing answers about Canaan. The nurse stated his
name and said, *"I need to know what is wrong with Canaan?"*

I sat on the other end of the phone in a confused state
of mind, wondering what was going on. I asked the nurse,
*"Did the hospital transfer all of Canaan's records and x-rays
with him?"*

His reply was, *"Yes, they did."*

I then asked, *"Did Canaan's x-rays not show he had a hole in his lung?"*

He replied, *"Yes, it did. However, when he arrived at the hospital, we did our own x-rays. It no longer shows one. He's breathing fine!"*

Because the hospitals are only fifteen minutes apart, I knew God had healed our son in those few early-morning hours.

I then asked, *"Can we come pick him up?"*

His reply was, *"He cannot leave until the seventy-two-hour culture comes back negative, with no other problems. Only then will he be able to go home."*

Three days later, all was good. He came home with no problems, except waking up every two hours wanting a bottle. As soon as I went to sleep, he would wake back up wanting to be fed again. I quickly became exhausted since I wasn't able to get much sleep at night, which comes with having a newborn baby, of course. Other than sleep deprivation, everything was going fine...until three weeks later.

Early one morning, I had just finished feeding Canaan and laid him on his back in the bassinet. I then laid down in my bed, which was beside his bassinet. About five minutes had passed when I heard God say, *"Look at Canaan."* At that moment, as soon as my eyes peeked into the bassinet, I saw him projectile vomit. Throwing up with so much force was something I had never before seen, and he was my third child!

Every time I tried to feed him that morning, he threw it up. I knew something was seriously wrong. So we went to see his pediatrician, which was an hour away. By the time we arrived, he had become as limp as a dishrag and was no longer crying. She admitted him to the hospital. My only thought was, *I don't know if I can handle much more of this, my baby is hysterically crying because he's hungry. I feel helpless because I can't feed him.*

I started to rock him and pray out loud, *"Jesus, please take his hunger away and let him go to sleep."*

I could tell that the more he cried, the weaker he became. My husband asked if he needed to come to the hospital, but I told him, *"Stay at work. We can't afford to lose a paycheck, and you couldn't do anything anyway."* I didn't need more stress on me than what I already had. When my friend, Rhonda, found out Canaan was in the hospital, she came to help me.

The heartfelt counsel of a friend is as sweet as perfume and incense. Proverbs 27:9 | NLT

The next day, they finally figured out what was wrong with him. He had pyloric stenosis, a rare condition that makes the pylorus valve, which is sitting between a newborn's stomach and small intestine, become thick and narrow. It stays closed to hold food in the stomach, then it opens to release food in the intestine, where it is later digested. Pyloromyotomy, which is the surgery needed to fix the condition, is performed to remove the blockage.

After Canaan's surgery, the pediatrician said, *"He will be fine, the surgery took care of his problem."* However, three weeks later, Canaan started projectile vomiting again.

I've heard it said that God won't put any more on you than you can handle. However, by this point, I was seriously wondering!

I called the pediatrician and told her, *"Canaan has pyloric stenosis again."*

Her reply was, *"Mrs. Spann, I've been a doctor for over thirty years. I've never heard of a baby having this twice. That surgery fixed your son's problem; it's gone!"*

I assuredly replied, *"I'm telling you he has it again."*

She then said, *"Mrs. Spann, I'm going to request another upper gastrointestinal series (UGI) test to prove to you he does not have pyloric stenosis again. After the test is over, go sit in the waiting room until I call."*

I was in the room with Canaan where they were performing the UGI test. As I was feeding him his bottle with the barium, I watched the x-ray monitor to see if it emptied out of his tummy. Of course, the technician would not tell me anything. However, I had been through this before, and I could see it was not emptying out.

I went to the waiting room, anxiously waiting for the pediatrician's call to verify my fears. I waited about thirty minutes until a nurse came to me and asked, *"Mrs. Spann?"*

I replied, *"Yes."*

She said, *"You have a phone call at the nurse's desk. Please follow me."*

When I got to the nurse's desk, I answered the phone, *"Hello."*

It was the doctor. *"Mrs. Spann, I'm so sorry! Canaan's test was positive for pyloric stenosis."*

I burst into tears. I couldn't understand why this was happening to me! If there was a bad Twilight Zone, I felt I was in it.

I kept thinking, *God, WHY do I have to go through all of this? What reason?* I felt as if God was testing my Faith. I would have to say, I wasn't prepared at all for this particular journey.

Once again, Canaan was admitted to the hospital. The pediatrician called the doctor who performed his first surgery and found out he had just caught an airplane and was flying out of the state. He would be gone for a week, and there was no one else in Monroe, LA that did that kind of surgery on babies. I thought, *Oh, God. Can this get any worse!*

Our only other option was LSU Medical Center in Shreveport, Louisiana. They took Canaan and me by ambulance. Shreveport is about two hours and forty-five-minutes from where we lived. I knew no one in Shreveport; we were alone. Again, I didn't want my husband to lose a paycheck, causing more problems, so I felt I had to do this by myself.

The doctor started with an ultrasound. He stated, *"I want to do an upper GI to make sure I see a blockage."* Once again, I stood there for the third time. Canaan started to drink the barium, and it did not empty out of his tummy as it should. We got back to his room and two doctors came in to confirm what I already knew and feared.

Surgery would be in the morning. The doctor stated, *"We will give Canaan some medicine to help calm his tummy, and we will see you in the morning."* It was Wednesday, and also church night. I called Brother Geary and told him, *"Canaan is back in the hospital at LSU. Please pray for him at tonight's service."*

My husband, Gary, and his mother, Janie, drove to see Canaan, stayed for a few hours and then went home. That night, I prayed desperately that God would heal Canaan. I needed this to be over one way or another so I could get back home.

The next morning, the doctors came back in the room to talk to me before Canaan's surgery. They asked, *"How did he do last night with the medicine we gave him?"*

I answered, *"He did fine."*

One of the doctors said to me, *"Mrs. Spann, I feel strongly about doing another upper GI."*

I replied, *"Okay."* We went back to the room for another upper GI—for the *fourth* time. After Canaan finished drinking the barium, I stood there watching the monitor, and to my surprise, his tummy was emptying out.

I didn't need the technician to tell me this time; it was plain as day. Back to the room we went. The doctors came in to assure me that there would be NO surgery because the medicine from last night helped with opening the valve. The doctor then informed me that Canaan would have to take medicine thirty minutes before every meal for the rest of his life. I was sitting there so relieved that there would be no surgery! Then I started to think to myself, *How is being on medicine for the rest of your life good?*

A couple of weeks later, I had to go out for a few hours, so Gary kept Canaan. I left the instructions to Canaan's medicine, which included when and how much to give. As I walked out the door, I said, *"Do not forget to give him his medicine!"* Well, I guess I was speaking to the walls because Gary did not do anything I said. When I got home, I went straight to the cabinet where Canaan's medicine was. It had not been moved from where I left it that morning. I asked Gary, *"Did you not give Canaan his medicine thirty minutes before feeding him?"*

His reply was, *"No, I didn't!"*

I again asked, *"Did he throw up after you fed him?"*

He said, *"No, he didn't!"*

I was standing there trying to figure out what was going on because the doctors said Canaan would have to be on the medicine for the rest of his life. My thought at that very moment was, *I'm also not going to give it to him! I don't want him to have to be dependent on this medicine for the rest of his life. Maybe being on the medicine for a few weeks fixed the problem. What if the doctors were wrong?*

Months passed. It was a Sunday morning, and the church was full. I was sitting there when suddenly I heard God say, *"Leisa, I want you to go up to the front and give your testimony of when I healed Canaan twice."*

Well, my very first thought was, *"Not again, God! You know I hate getting in front of a crowd of people."* But then I said, *"Twice God? When was the second time?"*

I then heard God say, *"Leisa, it was I who opened the valve, not the medicine you gave him."*

I started crying, because for weeks I had been giving the Glory to the medicine and not God. When you stop to think about it, if the medicine could open the valve, wouldn't all doctors use it instead of putting newborns under anesthesia for an operation?

I had believed the medicine was what healed Canaan instead of God, maybe because that answer was more practical than a MIRACLE!

That just built my faith even more. I knew now why I had to go through all I went through. God wanted to show me He was in control and that I should not put him in a box. If I'm going to pray for a miracle, I need to believe in receiving one.

All these years later, I'm convinced more than ever that the feeling I had while pregnant with Canaan was true. When he was a teen, three different evangelists revealed this to Canaan: God was going to use him in a great way!

CHAPTER 4

Anoint Me, Please

Every Sunday morning, church starts off with Praise and Worship singing. Most of the time, after I get finished singing and praising the Lord, my makeup is streaking down both of my cheeks; my mascara runs right along with my nose. I shouldn't take time to even put my makeup on because this happens almost every time. I can feel the Holy Spirit around me. I can't explain the feeling. All I can say is it's a very POWERFUL PRESENCE!

On one particular Sunday, the preaching started as usual, and at about 11:15 a.m. I heard God say, *"Leisa, pray for Aunt Bee!"*

I whispered to God, *"Okay, God. What's wrong with Aunt Bee?"*

God replied, *"Just pray, Leisa."*

I began to pray, blocking out everything else. I finished praying and thought it was all good, so my mind went back to the sermon. At about 11:50 a.m., only thirty minutes later, I heard God say, *"Leisa, I want you to go to the front and ask Brother Geary to anoint you with oil and you both pray for Aunt Bee."*

God said it with such authority that it seemed quite urgent. Naturally, I became a little concerned because I had just prayed a little earlier for Aunt Bee and felt all was good.

However, after Brother Geary closed with the Invitation Call, I went up to the front and said to him, *"God told me to come to the front and have you anoint me with oil and both of us pray for Aunt Bee."*

Brother Geary asked, *"Who's Aunt Bee?"*

I replied, *"She's the door greeter at Walmart. (She's not really my aunt. All the associates at Walmart call her that because she resembles Aunt Bee from the Andy Griffith Show.) And I don't know what's wrong with her."*

That's when Brother Geary said, *"Well, it doesn't really matter who Aunt Bee is, God knows what's wrong. So if He told you to do this, we have to be obedient and do it."*

Brother Geary anointed me, and we prayed. This is called an intercessory prayer, which is an act of praying on behalf of others. I stood in for Aunt Bee, filling in the gap as if she was there herself being anointed and prayed for.

> *Are any of you sick? You should call for the elders of the church to come and pray over you, anointing you with oil in the name of the Lord. Such a prayer offered in faith will heal the sick, and the Lord will make you well.*
> *James 5:14-15 | NLT*

A few days passed, and I was at work in the jewelry department where I was the manager. I had to go to the front of the store to get a shopping cart to fill with incoming freight. (After getting the cart, I always took it to the back door where the freight comes in.) As I was on my way to retrieve the cart, I could see Aunt Bee standing there at her post as door greeter.

I wanted to tell her Brother Geary and I prayed for her Sunday morning at church and hoped everything was okay. However, I heard God say, *"Don't tell her what you did, just ask her if there was anything wrong with her Sunday morning."*

So when I pulled my cart out, I said, *"Aunt Bee, was there anything wrong with you Sunday morning?"*

Aunt Bee replied, *"Oh, Leisa. I was sick as a dog! I woke up Sunday morning throwing up. I couldn't stop; it was constant. I was on the schedule to work, but I had to call in sick. However, around 12:00 p.m. I stopped throwing up. I felt so much better that I even called Walmart back and told them I could come to work."*

Wow! I stood there stunned over what she had just told me. I couldn't believe what I was hearing. I looked at her and said, *"Aunt Bee, let me tell you what happened to me Sunday morning."*

As I told her the story of how God wanted me to pray for her and then followed that up with explaining about being anointed, filling in the gap for her, she was astonished.

With tears rolling down her cheeks, she grabbed me up and gave me a big bear hug saying, *"Leisa, I've seen the changes in your life firsthand, and you have no idea how much you inspire me. The things that God has done in your life I've never heard before."*

I walked away once again, flying higher than a kite, yet having taken no drugs!

I SAID A PRAYER FOR YOU TODAY

I said a Prayer for you today
and I asked the Lord above.
To whisper into your ear
that someone sends their love.
I didn't ask for material things
for that's not important to me.
But I asked him to give you Faith
for things you wouldn't see.
I asked him to give you strength
so you could endure anything.
And I asked for you a measure of Hope
for the Victory that this will bring.
©Leisa Spann

CHAPTER 5

A Sign from God

In May of 2000, God told me to quit my job at Walmart, open up an inspirational gift shop in my hometown of Oak Grove, Louisiana, and call it Just a Touch of Heaven. At that point in time, I thought, *God, that's a crazy idea!* It seemed like everyone who opened up a small business in Oak Grove didn't make it, closing down within a year or two.

At the time, I had worked full time for thirteen years at Walmart, making almost ten dollars an hour plus benefits, which was a very good income in Oak Grove back then. In addition, I had a retirement plan and all kinds of insurance—more that I would ever need. Without fail, I knew how much my paycheck would be every two weeks, which was a great blessing.

After I told God that opening a store was a crazy idea, I said to him, *"God, are you kidding me? You want me to give up my paycheck, my health, dental, and life insurances, plus go to the bank and borrow $35,000 and Trust You?!? Why would I want to quit my job and open up something that would put my family in hardship? What if it doesn't work?"*

I then thought about one of my favorite scriptures. I never really thought this is what it meant to Trust God—leaning on Him when I did not understand!

Trust in the Lord with all your heart; do not depend on your own understanding. Seek His will in all you do, and He will show you which path to take. Proverbs 3:5-6| NLT

I began to pray and seek God more after He brought this thought to my mind.

I told God, "You give me a sign, and if this is Your will, then I will do whatever you want me to do. It will not matter that I will no longer have a paycheck or benefits because I know you will take care of my family and me."

About five weeks later, I went to Gayle's restaurant in Oak Grove where I was supposed to meet someone to pick up a package. As I drove up, I noticed that the person's car was not there. Thinking I had missed the person I had planned to meet, I still got out of my vehicle and went to the door not expecting it to open. When I pulled back on the door handle, to my surprise, it opened. I walked inside.

Instead of the person that I was supposed to meet, there was another worker inside. She knew that I wrote poetry, framed the poems, and sold them to gift shops around Northeast Louisiana. She told me that she had seen some of my framed poetry and said they were beautiful and asked me how they were doing. I shared with her that God had opened up all kinds of doors.

I told her, "What's crazy is that now God wants me to open up a Christian gift shop and put a waterfall inside and not a just a tabletop waterfall but a big waterfall."

I continued, *"I have not figured that one out yet."*

Then I noticed that her eyes got really big. She seemed excited and said, *"Oh my, you are Leisa."*

I thought, "What a strange thing for her to say." She ran to the counter and got a little, spiral, black notebook and began flipping through the pages.

She said, *"God gave me three things to pray for the other day. I wrote them in this book so I would not forget to pray for them. One of the names was Leisa, and I had no idea which Leisa I was to pray for."*

She showed me the three names she had written down in the book. However, the spelling was not Leisa but Lisa, which is the most common way to spell it. Tears began trickling down my cheek.

She looked at me and said, *"Now, as far as the waterfall goes, you know, Jesus is the Living Water, and the well never runs dry."*

By that time, I had started fully crying, my hair stood straight up on the back of my neck, and I thought, *"Okay, God, that is all the sign I need."* Wow!

The worker that day was Jeani. Not only did He give me a sign, but He used Jeani to give it to me. You remember Jeani, right? She was the woman in *"Finding My Purpose"* when God used me a few years earlier as she acknowledged Jesus that Sunday morning. I knew this was God's will for me and this was what He wanted me to do.

To God I said, "I will quit my job at Walmart and open up this Christian gift shop because I know this is Your will and Your will is what I want to do." And that was that. My last day at Walmart was Oct. 30, 2000.

I opened up my Christian gift shop on December 1 of that same year. On the day of my grand opening, my friend, Liz, gave me a gift: a thirty-inch tall, silver cross. I thought about how beautiful and wonderful it would look on the wall behind my register where all my customers would see it.

I then heard God say, "You will have a cross on that wall, but that one is not it. Your cross will be bigger, and you will have a spotlight on your cross at night."

So I thought, "Okay, God. Whenever it's time, I know you will tell me where I am supposed to purchase this cross."

After Christmas, Walmart always runs an after-Christmas sale, and that year they had a spotlight for 50% off. I remembered what God had told me in the fall, so I bought the spotlight thinking to myself, *When it's time to purchase my cross, I will already have my spotlight.*

One day my mother, Nancy, and her four sisters were spending time together and decided to come by the store. They were at the front looking at gift items when I called Mary Jean, the youngest of the five sisters, to the back to show her something.

In the back of the store, I had a newspaper clipping from the ribbon cutting ceremony from the store's opening. Earlier, I had noticed something quite amazing in the picture from the clipping, but had yet to mention it to anyone, not even my mother. I showed Mary Jean the article with the picture and asked her to identify everyone she knew in the picture. She started naming everyone she saw. As she was rattling off names, she stated, *"There's Daddy, my Papaw,"* and continued naming others.

I stopped her and reminded her that I had opened on December 1, 2000, and Papaw (her dad) passed away August 9, 1998. Mary Jean immediately burst into tears and called her sisters one by one to the back including my mom—Nancy, Aunt Poochie, Aunt Dinky, and Aunt Mamie Lee. Mary Jean showed them the newspaper of the ribbon cutting ceremony and asked each one who they saw. As each sister named the participants, they each included their dad. Mary Jean reminded each sister that was impossible as he had been gone for a few years. They were all in shock over what they saw!

Papaw was in the very back part of the picture, just his head and shoulders—no body or legs. We could account for everyone else there, seeing their bodies and legs, but not his. The significance of this comes from a poem I wrote at 3:00 a.m. the morning after he passed away.

At this point in my life, I had never written a poem before. After waking up and writing this first poem, I read it back to myself and started crying, thinking to myself, *Why did I wait until after he passed away to express my love for him.*

I sat there with tears rolling down my cheeks and said to God, *"God, I feel I need to write poetry and do it so others can let their loved ones and friends know how much they mean to them. If you give me the poems and tell me how to go about doing this, I want to be used in this way."* So when I saw my Papaw in the picture of the ribbon cutting ceremony, and he being the reason I started writing poetry in the first place, I knew IT WAS A GOD THING!

CHAPTER 6

The Cross

The first week in February, after the store opened, I was sitting at my small table next to the waterfall, reading my Bible, when I heard God say, *"It's time for His cross."* I thought He would then tell me where to purchase the cross, but that's not what He said.

God said, "The cross cannot be 2 two-by-fours nailed together. It has to be big, and it has to look old. Hang a robe on the cross. The material of the robe must be purple velvet or velveteen, and it must have trim around it with a crown of thorns at the top, and a sign that says:

"THIS IS JESUS, KING OF THE JEWS."

He told me to call Mike, who was a different carpenter than the one I hired to build my office in my store. After retrieving his number from the phone book, I called. There was no immediate answer, but Mike called me back a few hours later. I told him I had a project for him and that I wanted a large cross on my wall. So he came to my shop to see what exactly I needed.

When he arrived, I explained, *"Okay, I am going to tell you just like God told me. It cannot be just 2 two-by-fours nailed together. It has to be big, and it has to look old."*

He looked at me and with a sarcastic attitude said, *"How do you make a piece of wood look old?"*

At this point, I was thinking, *"Okay, God, not only did you tell me that the wood had to look old, you told me which car-penter to call. So, what's your plan for the wood?"*

I looked at the carpenter and said, *"I have no idea how to make a piece of wood look old. You are the carpenter, and God told me to call."*

He said, *"Okay, I'll figure something out as to how or what I can do to make it look old."* Then he said, *"How big—four-by-four or six-by-six?"*

I replied, *"I have no idea. I will have to see it."* So he went home to get a piece of four-by-four and a piece of six-by-six. When he came back with the wood, I immediately pointed to the six-by-six, *"That's it!"* He looked at me and then at the wall, knowing there was sheetrock throughout the whole store. He then looked back at me and said, *"There is no way you are going to get a piece of four feet long and six inches by six inches in diameter to hang on this wall. It will be entirely too heavy; you will have to have something to bolt that thing to."*

Well, I knew that God did not tell me to do all of this for it not to work, so I said, *"You go get the material and make the cross. We won't worry about how we are going to hang it until later."* So he left and went to the lumber yard about 20 miles away.

About an hour later, Mike walked back into the store and said, *"You are never going to believe this. You have to come look."*

"What?" I replied.

While we were walking outside to take a look, Mike explained, *"All the way to the lumber yard, I was trying to figure out what I was gonna do because I didn't believe what you wanted would ever work. When I got there, I was talking to a sales clerk about how I could maybe find a cross made out of styrofoam, but that would only solve one problem. I still had to do something to make it look old. Someone overheard me say that and chimed in, 'We have a piece of sixteen-foot long, six-by-six cedar wood that has been laying on the ground outside for over twenty years.'"*

When I walked out of the gift shop and saw the piece of cedar that Mike brought back, it had cracks, it had holes, and it looked old. Once again my hair stood straight up.

He looked at me and said, *"Now, it's sixteen-feet long so I can make it ten feet tall from the floor to the ceiling, and the floor will support the weight."*

I looked at him and said, *"I don't think this is just a co-incidence—you going to the lumber yard and someone telling you about this sixteen-foot long, six-by-six piece of cedar wood that has been laying out there for over twenty years. God knew where that piece of cedar wood would end up and its purpose, right here in this store."*

WOW! I thought. *Cedar wood—how awesome is that?!?*

For God to make His cross, it had to be cedar wood. One only has to look to Jesus Christ to understand God's interest in choice of materials concerning the temple. Everything God gave us on the earth will boldly lead to the only begotten Son of God. In this case, the focus was cedar. Why cedar?

Cedar is a strong evergreen that is not subject to corruption. Insects or worms do not threaten cedar.

The tall evergreen also yields fruit or cone. What is unique about cedar is that the root and cone produce a gum that gives a balsamic fragrance. When the tree is harvested, the wood is red in color. Cedar was not only used in the construction of the Temple but was also used in the sacrificial and ceremonial process of cleansing the leper in the Old Testament.

Like the evergreen that keeps its leaf green with life year round, Jesus was given to this world with life itself in His being. The Bible says that He was a root out of dry ground, meaning His Father was not of this world. He did not suffer the corruption, which death normally delivers because He rose from death three days after the fact.

Following the baptism with the Holy Ghost, Jesus demonstrated the power of God daily during His ministry. The Holy Ghost typifies the oil or gum from the cedar. As previously stated, when cedar is cut, it produces a red-colored wood. The red blood of Jesus Christ dying on the wooden cross cleanses whosoever will call upon the name of the Lord in faith.

Leprosy was a terrible disease that corrupted the flesh of whoever had it. A sacrificial ceremony containing two clean birds, scarlet, hyssup, and cedar was the requirement of the Law.

Today, if a believing sinner comes to God with faith in Jesus Christ, the corruption of sin and death will be swallowed up with the Life of Christ. Then the Holy Spirit will yield His fruit in the newborn Christian. And that believer will grow on earth, but be rooted in heaven. The Bible refers to salvation in a believer as a sweet smelling odor to God. No wonder God used cedar for the cross in my store.

When Solomon finished building the Temple, the entire inside, from floor to ceiling, was paneled with wood.

He paneled the walls and ceilings with cedar.
1 Kings 6:14-15 | NLT

All this happened on a Thursday, and I immediately called the company The Crown of Thorns to order the particular crown of thorns to put on the top as God instructed me to do.

On the following Saturday morning when I drove up to the store, I saw that Mike was waiting for me. He had finished the cross, and it was ready for the wall. Looking at the cross, knowing that it had been aging for over twenty years to be in my store was just awesome. I paid and thanked him for a wonderful job, and he went on his way.

After the cross was on display, I asked a customer in the store to guess about how many yards of material I would need for the robe I was going to hang on the cross. She told me about five or six yards. God told me that the material had to be purple velvet or velveteen. I pulled out my big telephone book and looked up every fabric shop in the yellow pages within a 100-mile radius of where I lived. I had a feeling I was going to have to call every one of them before I found purple velvet or velveteen material.

The first store I called was in Monroe, Louisiana. I told them who I was, that I was from Oak Grove, and that I was looking for purple velvet or velveteen. I asked them if they had any. I was going to let her know that I needed five or six yards, but the lady had already laid the phone down to search for it.

She came back and said, *"Ma'am we have exactly five yards on a bolt."*

I replied, *"Oh, my gosh. That is exactly what I need!"*

You should have seen me. I was jumping up and down for joy. The very first fabric store I called had just exactly what I needed, so I told the lady to please save it for me and that I would be over there in a few days to pick it up.

The following Monday, I asked a friend to watch the store for me while I went to Monroe to pick up the fabric. Monroe is about sixty miles from where I live. When I got over there, they pulled out the fabric from under the counter and it was the most awesome, richest looking color of purple I had ever seen. It was gorgeous. Let's not forget God said that it had to have trim, so I headed to the trim department. I picked up a gold, filigree-type trim, and I carried it over to the lady.

She said, *"Hun, that is not enough trim to go all the way around the material that you have picked out."*

So I went back and looked again. That was the most trim that they had. I thought, *God, I don't know what to do.*

I looked around and saw a roll of intertwining purple and gold rope. God told me to buy the whole roll. I thought, *Now, God, I did take home economics in school and I do know that this is round and it is a rope and it can't be sewn on as the trim. I don't think that is going to work.*

He said, *"Buy it, the whole roll."*

So, of course, I took it to the lady and when she asked how many yards I needed, I told her the whole roll. Well, I got a funny look as she was rolling it off and measuring. I bought both the whole bolt of material and the whole roll of decorative rope and went to my car.

When I got into my car, I called my friend who was working at the store, and she told me she had been very busy and would I please hurry up and get back. I told her that I hadn't found my trim yet, and I had to do it that day. And off I went to another store to look for some trim.

I arrived at the next fabric store and opened up a McCall's pattern book. As I was flipping through the pages, I saw something purple that had some black and gold trim with the Greek key pattern on it. How awesome! I thought, *Yes, God, this is what you want me to get.* However, when I checked, there was only a small amount of the trim on the roll. By this time I was getting frustrated because I hadn't found any trim for the robe that God told me it needed. As I stood there almost in tears, I started thinking, *I don't know what you want me to get, God.*

Just then I looked down and saw a whole roll of the same pattern made with white and gold with the Greek key pattern. All of a sudden I knew that was what I was supposed to get. I purchased it immediately and headed back to Oak Grove. The next morning, I took it to my seamstress and told her how I wanted it sewn on, and she said that she could do it. Later on that day, the Crown of Thorns I purchased arrived, and I put them on the cross.

That evening, my seamstress finished sewing the robe and brought it to me. I climbed up on the ladder and I put the purple velvet robe, trimmed with white and gold, on the cross. As I looked at the finished product, I was in awe. It looked simply beautiful and worthy of Jesus. As I looked down, I saw the rope and thought I would just take it back. I still didn't know why God wanted me to buy that rope anyway. However, for no reason, I picked up the rope, rolled some off, and I flipped it over the middle and let some of it fall in the creases on the robe. When I did that, I thought, *Oh, my gosh, this looks amazing.* The rope became the finishing touch that I didn't know I needed. I used the whole roll and had about 3½ inches left over. Again, I marveled at how God let me buy just enough.

Several days later, I was wondering why God had me buy such expensive materials and why he wanted it this specific way. I already knew they had put a purple robe on Jesus, but that was all I knew. So I began studying the type of robe they put on him. I pulled my King James Bible out and read it. Matthew stated that they had put a *scarlet* robe on Jesus. Mark stated that it was purple, and Luke said that it was a gorgeous robe. I did not know the definition for scarlet in Bible times so I looked the word up in my Smith Bible Dictionary. It said to go to colors, which stated: *artificial mixtures which were employed in dyeing or painting. The purple and blue were derived from a small shellfish found in the Mediterranean, and were very costly, and hence they were the royal colors.* This was exactly what God had me make: an expensive, gorgeous robe of royal colors.

I was overwhelmed with the final outcome—the wood being cedar and having laid outside at a lumberyard for over twenty years, the robe being gorgeous and expensive. After studying the Bible, I understood all that God wanted me to do and the reason for it. From time to time, I would see customers in my store just stand and stare at the cross. I saw a lady staring at it one day who finally said, *"That is the most gorgeous thing I have ever seen."* She continued, *"I even see seven ropes hanging on the robe."* I had not realized that until she pointed it out, but if you counted both sides and the middle, they added up to the number seven.

In the Bible, seven was often referred to as God's perfect number and the number of completion. Seven was mentioned numerous times in the Bible. John spoke of the seven miracles that Jesus performed, and Jesus said seven things while he was on the cross.

You know, sometimes I feel that God has me do some crazy things. And through each of them, He wants to see how obedient I will be and how far I will go for Him.

From day one of opening my store, God has given me testimony after testimony, miracle after miracle. I feel that if we walk in the perfect will of God every day and ask Him every day to use us in whatever way He chooses, He will continue to bless us and use us.

I ask him daily to use me to minister to others. I think we should share the everyday miracles that God performs in our lives.

How far will you go for Him?

For the miracles He performs in my life—God has also given me a poem to share about the cross. I hope that everybody who wears a cross around their neck, on their arm, or in their ear, will realize the significance of it and how it came to be.

THE CROSS

Do you remember the cross and how it came to be,
that God's only son Jesus died on Calvary?
The stripes they put upon His back were not made of clothes.
But scars from strikes that day were awful, painful blows.
He wore upon His head a crown not made of gold.
For His was made of thorns, with cuts, the blood just rolled.
The robe was purple in color, gorgeous in every way.
The soldiers mocked and spit on Him, oh, what a price to pay.
With nails in His hands and feet hanging from that tree.
We were on His mind that day; He died for you and me.
©Leisa Spann

CHAPTER 7

A Friend in Prayer

The month prior to the store's opening, God gave me a sign that this store wasn't going to be a normal place where people come to shop. Instead, it was to be a place where people would come for prayer, healing, or just to feel the presence of God.

I knew I wouldn't be getting paid, so I didn't feel it was a job like what I had at Walmart. However, I fully understood after what happened the month before opening that it wasn't about me selling inspirational gifts, but about being a true servant for the Lord.

Even though I didn't see the full picture at the time, He had been preparing me for what was to come. In November, a few weeks before I was to open the store, I encountered God in a big way. My circle of friends and I, which mostly consisted of Walmart employees, were at Johnny's Pizza playing pokeno; this is a game kinda like bingo, having twelve players. We would have a drawing once a year to see which one of us would be the hostess for each month.

As a part of this group, all twelve players paid ten dollars every month, and the hostess then bought four gifts with the money and prepared a meal of her choice. First place earned a forty-dollar gift. The person who won the most games that night chooses the gift they want. Second place earned a thirty-dollar gift, which meant they got to choose next. Third place was a twenty-dollar gift, which meant they got what was left over. Then there was the booby gift, which was for the person who won the least amount of games that night.

We would get together the first Tuesday of every month at the hostess's house or wherever they chose to have it. It was really just a night out without the kids and husbands, a night of fun and laughter with beloved friends and family. The hostess for November 7, 2000 chose to have it at our local Johnny's Pizza. However, this certain night, about halfway through our evening, an employee came and told us they were shutting down early because of a death in the owner's family. We all looked at each other wondering, *What are we going to do now?* We had eaten our meal, which was pizza, but we still had many games to finish. So I jumped up and said, *"Hey, we can go to my store and finish the games. I have brown paper covering up all the windows, and no one can see inside. I have new carpet, and we can sit on the floor and finish playing."*

Everyone looked at me and agreed, so we picked up everything and headed over. We arrived at the store, and I found a place to sit right under where my music was going to be with my back against the wall and my card laid out in front of me on the floor. We had already played most of the games when I heard a loud, stern voice say to me, *"HOW DARE YOU GAMBLE IN THE HOUSE OF THE LORD!"*

What did I just hear? And then I heard it again—as if once wasn't enough! It scared the Heebie-Jeebies out of me.

I was trying to figure out what I did wrong, what was going on, and why God was so angry with me. If you had heard what I heard, you would have been scared, too.

Then I heard God say, *"You are not to ever play again."* I was clearly no longer in the game as my mind was talking to God and processing what He said.

I said, *"But God, next month is my month to be the hostess. I can't just quit now."*

God replied, *"You can find someone to take your place, and you can still be the hostess next month, after which you're done."* WOW! I sat there wondering how in the world I was going to explain this encounter to all the others who were with me.

As I sat there pondering for a minute or two what I was going to say, I came to realize there was no other way to explain it other than exactly how it happened. I thought if some chose to not believe me then that was their problem. I started by saying, *"I've got something to say..."* My words didn't want to come out as I was still shaken up over what happened. I told my friends the story as I was sitting there playing pokeno with them.

When I finished, Sharri said, *"I knew something was going on with you. I could tell you weren't in the game at all, your mind was miles away, and your face was as white as a sheet!"*

I hadn't realized until that moment that my fear of God could be seen on my face; I felt the fear all over my body, that's for sure. At that moment, I felt what God-fearing really meant. What was so amazing was that when I finished telling everyone what happened, all the members, one by one said, *"I'm done after December too."*

None of us realized that what we were doing was a form of gambling at the time. It was something for us to do every month for fun with friends and family. So you see, God was getting me ready to serve Him, a true servant for the days to come. He knew that everything I did in public would be watched by others. God had to cut everything out of my life that wasn't good in His eyes. He was going to give me a ministry, and the store was like the church as far as God was concerned.

I now realized He had given me a great responsibility.

Even though I no longer worked at Walmart, I was right next door, in the same parking lot; my friends would come to see me and eat lunch with me from time to time. This is when my ministry really began. At the time, I still only saw it as a store, never knowing God's plans for my life.

I soon realized, however, His exact plans for me as a part of His ministry when I heard the store's doorbell go off when a customer walked in. She came to a stop after she walked in, standing inside the front door. I looked up to notice this customer was someone I knew from childhood. All of a sudden, she said, *"I have no idea why I'm here, I was on my way to Walmart."* It was at that time when I heard God say, *"Witness to her."*

I started telling her my story, and she stood there with tears rolling down her cheeks. She ran to me and gave me a big bear hug, thanking me.

At the time I was thinking, *What did I do?* All I did was open my mouth and talk; this is something I'm good at. However, it was not my words that pierced her heart; God was in total control while I was testifying. It was something she needed to hear.There was POWER in those words, and God had redirected her path that day to walk into my store. She needed something that no one could give her but God.

I didn't fully understand what was going on until she stated she was addicted to drugs. I told her that she didn't have to tell me, but she felt she needed to for whatever reason. And I still had no idea what God wanted me to do besides witness to her. Then God told me to give her a certain book from my book section. So I walked to where all the books were and pulled it off the shelf. I told her God wanted her to read this book.

I know what you're thinking, *Why would I take a brand new book off the shelf and give it to her?* I did it because God told me to, and I could no longer let money dictate my actions. Was I going to let money be my master, or the Lord? It was not an easy choice, and it's hard not to let money control us. However, I felt this was where I truly stepped into my ministry. I wasn't going to let money be an issue, and I truly believed this was also a test for me. I knew somehow, some way, God would replace the cost of the book with a blessing, I just didn't know how.

> *The seeds that fell on the good soil represent honest, good-hearted people who hear God's word, cling to it, and patiently produce a huge harvest. Luke 8:15 | NLT*

I believe God blesses those with a giving heart, but I also believe your heart has to be doing it for the right reasons and not for financial gain.

My childhood friend then took the book out of my hand, hugged me again, and walked out of the store. I didn't know if I would see her again or not. I just knew I did what God wanted me to, and it was now in His hands. The next day, I had my helper watch the store while I ran some errands. I called to see if everything was going okay, and she told me someone came in and left a book.

My thought was, *Oh, no! God, what went wrong?*

I had just given her the book yesterday evening, and she returned it this morning. I had never read this book, and I had no idea what the book was about. I was so worried and confused as to why she would bring the book back before she read it. The day after she brought the book back, she came back again to the store, and I've never been so glad to see someone in my life. She had a smile on her face and was glowing! I asked her, *"Why did you bring the book back before you read it?"*

Her reply was, *"I did read it. I was up all night reading it."*

Wow! I thought to myself. *That must have been a good book not to want to put it down.*

She said, *"I need to talk to you."* So we sat down at the table beside the waterfall in the store. She continued, *"When I was a teen, I had two abortions, and as an adult it has bothered me. The book you gave me comforted me about this, and I know my babies are in heaven. I can't go back and change what I did, but I know God has forgiven me."*

You watched me as I was being formed in utter seclusion, as I was woven together in the dark of the womb. Psalms 139:15 | NLT

"I've also been on drugs for a long time," she continued. *"I don't want to do this, but I just can't seem to stop. However, since leaving your store the first day I came in, I've not had a craving for any drugs in three days; the urge is gone."* It was at that point that I realized why God sent her to the store.

God has the POWER to take someone who is addicted to drugs, alcohol, pornography, cigarettes, food, sex, etc. and take the cravings away. We both sat there with tears rolling down our cheeks. I kept thinking, *How awesome are you, God?*

She hugged me and said, *"I will be back soon."* And left.

It was then that I heard God say, *"Take her under your wing and be the friend she needs. Hire her to help you with inventory after Christmas."* I thought that was a great idea, but just as soon as I thought it, guess who was ready to argue the situation? The devil jumped in full force by telling me it was NOT a good idea.

He reminded me that I just opened the store and would be closed down shortly after word got around that I had a worker here in a Christian gift shop who was battling a drug addiction. What would people say? I'll tell you what they would say, *"How dare you hire someone like that to work for you? I will shop somewhere else."*

I sat there thinking, *Who does this, God? What am I gonna do?*

The fight against good and evil was on! What God wanted me to do was crazy, but what the devil was saying was exactly what people would say. I said to God, *"Why would you strip me of all that was bad in my life to prepare me for this store and then want me to hire someone who does drugs?"*

I then heard God say, *"It's not a store that I gave you, Leisa. It's my ministry. I put you here to encourage those who need encouraging, to heal those who need healing, comfort those who need comforting, and to be a light in a world of darkness."*

I said, *"Okay, God. I will do Your will and trust You."*

I called her the next day, and she started working the first week in January. Her family members came into the store to thank me for what I had done. (My friend had gone straight to her mom's house and recounted the whole story about what had happened on the first day.) It was God's way of putting His arms around her and telling her, *"You're mine."*

I prayed for her often, even after she had finished helping me with inventory. She was always in my thoughts and prayers. One Sunday morning, I was getting ready for church and was sitting in the tub praying for her when all of a sudden God started giving me a poem.

I jumped out of the tub and got my paper and pen and wrote a poem for her. I thought I was writing this poem just for her, never knowing this would be one of my best-selling poems. One that others would want to buy for their friends as well. I believe this was my blessing for being obedient when God told me to witness and for taking her under my wing and being a true friend to her.

A FRIEND IN PRAYER

As I come to you, my Father,
in prayer once again, asking for your
help today for my special friend.
I'm asking that you guide her each and
every day, to give her strength and all
she needs to help along the way.
And when she's feeling lonely
and doesn't feel you care,
please put your arms around her
and let her know you're there.
I pray you send an angel that comes
from up above, to keep her safe in all
her ways and let her know she's loved.
©Leisa Spann

A Friend loveth at all times.
Proverbs 17:17 | NLT

CHAPTER 8

AC, Anyone?

One hot, summer day, my husband, Gary, called me from work saying, *"Hey, there's a guy here I'm working with who has a gun that I want, and this guy has a need. The man has a baby, and his air conditioner went out in his trailer. He doesn't have the money to buy one, and I thought maybe you could bless him with the air conditioner. He would then give me the gun as a trade."*

I was a little confused about what he was saying, so I confirmed. *"Let me get this straight, you want me to go buy this guy an air conditioner, and in return, you get his gun. Correct?"*

He said, *"Yes!"*

I couldn't believe my husband had just asked me to do this, even adding in the fact that the guy had a baby. I guess this was to make me feel some urgency because in Louisiana it's like a hot oven during the summer. I thought my husband was crazy. Air conditioners are expensive, and there are lots of people in Louisiana who don't even have them. I knew the real reason my husband called me; he wanted that gun. Period.

My first thought was that there was no way I would buy this guy an air conditioner. Then, after thinking about it, another thought came, *"What if this is a God thing?"*

After thinking about it, I said to my husband, *"First off, you are not getting the gun. That's not how God works! Second, if God wants me to buy an air conditioner for this guy, it will not matter to me how much it costs. I will buy it. I will pray and ask God to give me a sign to confirm this is what He wants me to do. Third, if God does give me a sign to buy the air conditioner, I do not want the guy to know who bought it!"*

But when you give to someone in need, don't let your left hand know what your right hand is doing. Give your gifts in private, and your Father, who sees everything, will reward you. Matthew 6:3-4 | NLT

I hung up the phone and prayed over the situation. The rest of the day, I thought someone might come into the store, saying something about an air conditioner.

After closing at 5:30 p.m., I drove home. As I walked in the house, my husband asked, *"Did God give you a sign?"*

I replied, *"No, I'm still praying about it, though. Maybe tomorrow."*

The next morning, I walked into the store, again asking God to give me a sign about the air conditioner. Every time the doorbell rang and a customer came in, I was expecting someone to say something about an air conditioner. Mid-morning, customers started coming in one after another. Just as soon as I checked one customer out and wrapped up their purchase another was standing in line at the register ready to be checked out. For a solid hour and a half, I was extremely busy, and I did not have time to think about an air conditioner. After the rush of customers ended and there was still no direct sign, I felt God wasn't going to give me one. In my heart, though, I knew He wanted me to buy this person the air conditioner.

My store was in a small town, I didn't receive a paycheck, and I had to TRUST GOD daily to provide me with sales to pay all the bills for the business. So paying hundreds of dollars for an air conditioner wasn't really in the picture. I only had about six hundred dollars in the store account and there were bills still needing to be paid.

However, this certain day, there was a rush of customers, which had never happened before except on a holiday. It was the middle of the summer, which is a very slow time for gift shops. I guess that's why I thought God wasn't going to give me a sign. After I convinced myself that God wasn't going to give me a sign, I called my husband to ask what size air conditioner I needed to buy. I knew a small window unit would not be big enough to cool a whole house or trailer in Louisiana.

I then called and enlisted my friend, Connie, who was working at Walmart's customer service desk. I asked her to bring the a/c unit to the front service desk and told her that I would run over to pay for it. Connie then agreed to call the person and let him know the package needed to be picked up.

As I got off the phone, I heard God say, *"Go pick out a card and tape it to the top of the air conditioner box when you pay for it."* I had over five hundred Inspirational Cards to choose from in the store. How in the world do I pick out the right card, one that God wants me to send?

I responded to God by saying, *"Okay, God, I'm going over to the five racks, one by one I'll point to each card going up and down the racks, and when I come to the card You want me to send, You tell me to stop."* I went over to the five standing racks of cards and started on the front side where three of the racks stood. After going through each rack, I continued around the back where the other two racks stood. As I searched the fourth rack, going up and down and turning each section of the rack, I began to think this method wasn't going to work. And then, all of a sudden, I heard God say, *"That's it!"* I reached for the card, pulled it out of the pocket, and thought, *Wow! What an awesome picture on the front.*

I walked over and laid the card down on the counter as God said, *"Underline the scripture on the front of the card."*

I grabbed a pen, and, without reading what it said, I underlined it. I didn't feel a need to read the card because, honestly, this card and what it said was clearly not meant for me, but for the person I was giving it to.

I then opened the card and wrote on the inside, *"This act of kindness is done through the love of God!"* I signed it with, *"Love and God Bless."*

I put the card in the envelope, locked the door to the store, and walked next door to Walmart. I paid for the air conditioner, taped the card to the top of the box, and handed Connie the piece of paper with the name and phone number of the man she was to call. I looked at her and said, *"Not one word of this to anyone."*

She responded, *"I promise. I won't tell a soul."*

Back to the store I went. I unlocked the door, and as soon as I walked inside, I said, *"Shooo, that was a lot of money. God, I sure hope that's what You wanted me to do, seeing how You didn't give me a sign."*

A few hours later, around closing time, my friend, Jamie, walked into my store with a box in hand, saying, *"Here."* She tossed the box at me and said, *"Someone at work told me to give you this because they want you to order puzzles for your store."* I caught the box, flipped it over to the front side, and let out an audible gasp at the picture on the front of the box. At that moment, I heard God say, *"Leisa, go back and read the scripture on the front of the card you sent."*

I was literally shaking all over. I couldn't believe what I was seeing. The front of the box had the exact picture on it that was on the front of the card God told me to send to the guy who I bought the air conditioner for a few hours earlier.

I walked over to the cards, picked up the particular one I had sent, and read what God had told me to underline. It was a scripture I never knew was even in the Bible.

Call unto me, and I will answer thee, and show thee great and mighty things. Jeremiah 33:3 | KJV

God then said, *"Leisa, instead of giving you a sign that you asked for, I've given you a testimony to share with the world."*

Wow, it's a God Thing!

CHAPTER 9

Tears in a Bottle

Did you know that God loves and cares for us so much that He bottles up our tears and records them in His book? That's right. The Word of God says that.

> **You keep track of all my sorrows. You have collected all my tears in your bottle. You have recorded each one in Your book. Psalms 56:8 | NLT**

We are God's creation—His children—and He wants the best for all of us. As a Father, why wouldn't He want to know all of our tears of sorrow? As a mother myself, if I could collect my children's tears and write them all down, I would. However, I know that's impossible for me.

But with God, all things are possible. Matthew 19:26 | [Translation here?]

One day, while working at the store, I was cleaning and dusting, and I decided to move some of the gift items around. Through the summer, sales are the lowest because people are on vacation, there are no holidays, and there is just not much going on after Father's Day. Because of this slowdown, I do not order inventory, so moving things around—something I learned at Walmart—helps keep the store and inventory looking updated.

This certain day, as I moved things around, I heard God say, *"Leisa, I want you to fast for forty days."* Yes, I stopped in my tracks and shook all over trying to convince myself that was not God! But then I heard God say it again. *"I want you to fast for forty days."* This time He added, *"You are not to eat anything after 3:00 p.m."*

Well, my thought at that second was, A*t least He didn't say forty days without ANYTHING to eat!*

Fasting wasn't new to me; I did it often. However, not for forty days. I sat down at the table to ponder on this for a little bit, trying to figure out why in the world God would tell me to do this. A lot of times, I try to figure God out. Yeah, I know. STUPID, right? However, I still try to, and as I sat at the table talking to God, I realized I wasn't going to figure this one out doing what I was doing.

I said to God, "Why God? Why would you tell me to do this when my last meal of the day is the hardest for me to do without? Plus, I have to go home and cook for my family. You mean I have to cook for the next forty days, look at the food, prepare the food, and smell the food as it lingers through my whole house—and I can't even eat?!?"

The longer I sat there, the longer I thought, I don't know if I can do this when I have no idea why I'm fasting. All the other times I fasted for a purpose...that I initiated—maybe for a healing, a certain prayer to be answered, or just a move of God in my life at the time. As I sat at the table in my little shop, I had an idea and said to God, "Okay, God. I will fast for you, and I will fast for me. It will be a 'hit two birds with one stone' situation." I needed to lose some weight, and Mama had always told me if I wouldn't eat anything after 5:00 in the evening, I would lose weight.

I thought to myself, If I can't eat anything after 3:00, surely I will lose 15 pounds at least by doing this. Yes, this is good.

About three weeks passed and I was still fasting when a customer came into the store asking if I had tear bottles. I told her I had never heard of tear bottles. She explained to me they were at one of the Christian gift shops in Monroe, LA, which was about sixty miles from my shop. I told my customer I would try and find some information about them and see about getting some for the store.

I called my friend, Sarah, who had a store in West Monroe who told me about a company that had tear bottles, and she gave me their information. They had a website, so I got on-line to see what this company offered, and I found their tear bottles. I had never seen anything like them before. At only two inches tall, the bottles were beautiful! So I decided to call the company and inquire.

Many companies out there have minimum order and re-order requirements. A lot of times, I would find something I wanted for the store and my first order had to be five hundred dollars or more to be able to stock it. Living in a small town made this too risky, so I often didn't order things I would love to have carried.

This time, however, the order requirements were not holding me back; it was the prices of the tear bottles. Yes, they were beautiful. I wanted them, but how many customers would actually buy them? Each bottle was individually boxed and had a card attached with the scripture from Psalm 56:8. I just couldn't see very many customers in my small town buying these two-inch bottles.

It was a beautiful idea. However, to me, it needed more meaning to make it sell. I even thought that if God gave me a poem, I could sell the tear bottles with a poem attached. But again, the price was just too high for me.

One morning, a few days later, I was in my bathroom put-ting on my makeup and thinking about the last five and a half weeks of fasting; I was on my thirty-seventh day. Not knowing why God wanted me to fast, and thinking I could fast for my own reason at the same time, I was feeling sorry for myself because I had no answer on why. And every morning when I got up, I weighed myself, and every morning it showed zero pounds lost! How was this possible? I didn't eat breakfast, and I only ate lunch and maybe a snack before 3:00 p.m.

I stopped what I was doing and said to God, *"God, why has the weight not come off? God, I thought this was going to be a 'hit two birds with one stone'? I would fast for you and fast for me. Am I not a good servant? God, I always give when you tell me to give. I've given my last five hundred dollars in my account before because I trusted you. When you told me to witness, I witnessed. God, why haven't you allowed me to lose weight? It's not like I'm asking for a million dollars!"*

As I stood still waiting for God to answer my question, in my mind, I sensed the answer wasn't going to be good for me, not one I wanted to hear anyway and surely not what I heard when He spoke next.

God answered back, *"Leisa, every time you got on the scale and saw you had not lost even one pound, you continued to fast for me. If I had allowed you to lose the weight, you would have gone from spiritual to the flesh, and you would have only continued to fast for yourself. You would have forgotten all about me."*

Wow! I stood there with my mouth gaping wide open, in shock at what I had just heard. And yet, as I think back to all the times I weighed myself, the disappointment was there, but I continued to fast for God without knowing the reason why?

That same day as I made it to the store about midday, I heard God say these words, *"Tears in a Bottle."* I sat down at my table with my notebook and pen, and God gave me the most beautiful poem. With every word I wrote, I felt it in my soul. God then whispered to me, Leisa, *"This is what you fasted for."* I realized God had given me something very special, and I needed to find my own bottles—making this offering my own.

TEARS IN A BOTTLE

This bottle is a gift that's a work of art.
It will hold your tears of sadness
from your broken heart.
God sends to us His angels that come from up above.
They carry a golden bowl that catches tears of love.
They're taken back to heaven, to the room of tears,
and poured into a bottle,
where there your name appears.
So when your heart is hurting
and some tears have fallen too,
remember that heaven's angels
have been surrounding you.
© Leisa Spann

God loves you so much; He bottles up every tear and records them in His book. He sees you tossing and turning through the night. His eyes never stray, night or day. He will give to those to reap in joy, who sowed in tears and what was sown in tears will come up a pearl. For the angels have the golden bowl that holds your prayers. The very day you call for help, the tide of battle turns. This one thing I know: God is for me!
Psalm 56:8-9 Psalm 126:5-6 Rev. 5:8

CHAPTER 10

Sending a Message

One morning I was in the bathroom getting ready for the day when I heard God tell me to pray for my friend, Maria. As usual, I immediately tried to figure out why I needed to pray for her. Maybe I do this so I will know what and how to pray. We all experience the same things in life, and I believe it's our duty as Christians to pray for one another. The trials we go through strengthen our own faith. And our testimonies can and will strengthen someone else's faith.

Even though I didn't know why God told me to pray for Maria, I acted on the prompting and started praying, covering everything I could think of that she may be going through. I finished praying and continued putting on my makeup.

When I got to the store that morning, as soon as I unlocked the door and crossed the threshold, I heard God say, *"Send Maria a card."*

I thought this meant to just send a card and let her know I was thinking of her and praying also. However, that wasn't the case because I then heard God say, *"I want you to write these words on the card."* Whoa, I thought!

I said, *"God, I've never done this before. You're telling me to give a message to someone, from you?! This is altogether different from giving a gift to someone from you or even witnessing to someone for you."* I stood there in disbelief and wondered if this was really God.

It is deep and scary to tell someone GOD said something, but I felt confident that it was God telling me to do this, so I conceded saying, *"Okay, God. I'm going to trust you and send Maria this message."*

I wrote what God wanted me to say on the card and sealed it up. I then picked up the phone to call her. When she answered the phone, I said, *"Maria, I have a message for you!"*

She replied, *"A message?"*

I said, *"Yes, a message, and please don't ask me what it is. I wrote it down for you, and I'm fixing to bring it to you."* Closing the store for a brief time, I delivered the card and then made my way back.

I waited.

And waited.

And waited some more…

Beside the phone for about fifteen minutes or so before deciding that she was not going to call. As I began to wonder, panic set in that maybe I had messed up. *Why hasn't she called me? She's had plenty of time to read what I wrote.*

Curiosity was getting the best of me, so I decided to call her. I picked up the phone to call, and then hung it back up. I thought, *Do I really want to know if I was totally wrong?!*

I was confident, however, that God sent me on this errand. So I picked up the phone again and called her. The phone rang, and I could hear Maria sobbing through the phone. At this point I was exploding with curiosity! I asked Maria with a little hesitation, *"Did the message I sent you from God make any sense to you?"*

Maria said, *"I've been praying for something for a long time, and when I got up this morning, I told God I wasn't going to pray for it anymore because obviously He wasn't going to an- swer my prayer. A few hours later, you sent me the card saying, 'Maria, God told me to tell you that it will come to pass, but you need to be still and wait on Him!'"*

Wow! Talk about a hair-raising, blow-me-away experi- ence. This didn't happen a week or even a day or two from her conversation with God. This happened the same day, the same morning, only a few hours from her final prayer on the matter. God wanted her to know, *"I hear you. Just give me time. I'm working on it."*

Be still, and know that I am God!
Psalms 46:10 | NLT

It is important for each of us to be obedient as soon as God directs us. We never know when or how He will use us, but if we are willing to act, He will definitely use us to bring to pass his purposes for others.

God did eventually answer Maria's prayer. However, it was in His timing, not hers.

I never asked Maria how much that experience increased her faith; I'm sure she was on a spiritual high for a while. It's very humbling to know God chose me once again, which increased my faith in God even more!

CHAPTER 11

Oh No, Not My Favorite

In early summer of 2002, a friend Viki and I were at the store, and a salesman from New York came in. In his hand, he held a medium-sized suitcase from which he sold sterling silver jewelry. He stated that he traveled all over the country selling sterling silver to stores. The man wanted to know if I would like to see his jewelry. Of course I said, *"Sure, I would love to see what you have."* We all sat down at a small table as he started pulling out beautiful pieces of jewelry, which included crosses, earrings, and pendants of all kinds.

All of his pieces were quite expensive, and I told him that I loved his jewelry, but due to the small town I lived in, I would never be able to markup the jewelry and sell it. I told him that

I would be glad to buy something for myself if he would let me purchase just one piece. Viki stated that she would buy a piece also, and he replied, *"Of course, you each could buy one piece."* I remembered seeing a gorgeous cross, which I loved. It was about three inches in length and full of sapphires, which happened to be my birthstone so I snatched it up right away. I was so excited to get that cross. It was different from any cross I had ever seen before—a one of a kind piece that I knew would be my favorite.

Later that summer, my husband, Gary, and I were getting ready to go to a church singing. The very last thing I do when getting dressed is put on my jewelry. I went to my jewelry box, opened it up, and began looking through all my crosses. I asked God, *"Which one should I wear tonight?"*

I heard Him say to me, *"Wear your favorite cross."*

I replied, *"That's a great idea. I've only worn it a few times."*

As I reached into my jewelry box and pulled it out, I started clasping it around my neck when God said, *"I am going to have you give that cross away tonight."*

I replied, *"Oh no—not my favorite! I've only had it for a short time, and I will never find another one like this, ever."* I continued, *"Okay, God. Let's compromise. I have a mother-of-pearl sterling silver cross right here. I've never worn it before, and I will give this one away."*

I reached into my jewelry box, pulled out the mother-of-pearl cross, and started to clasp it around my neck. However, my fingers could not pull back the clasp. It was as if my fingers froze. My heart sank. I took off the mother-of-pearl cross and then reached back into the jewelry box for my favorite.

I then said, *"Okay, God. The only way I will give this cross away is if someone stops me and says something about it. You know I've never had anyone stop me before over a piece of jewelry I was wearing. The chances of that happening are slim to none. In case I'm stopped, I'll give away my favorite cross. I'll know that's Your will and that I shouldn't hang on to material things of this world, believing You have something better for me."*

Gary and I went on our way to the singing, totally forgetting all about the conversation I had just had with God.

We drove up to the small church, got out of the truck, and walked up to the front doors. As we were about to enter, the female singer from the group walked up as well. At that moment, standing at the front doors of the church, I heard her say these words, *"That cross you have on is just gorgeous!"*

I smiled and said thank you, but my mind was saying, *Oh, My Gosh! She did not just say that to me!* I immediately said to God, *"Can I please wear it for a little while longer? I will give it to her after the singing is over."* Well, an hour and a half passed and the singing ended. It was time to take my cross off and give it to her. The lovely singer was standing at the table where they were selling their music. I walked up with my cross in hand and tried to give it to her. She said, *"I cannot take that!"*

Yes, that's really what I wanted to hear her say, but I knew in my heart I had to make her take it. I replied, *"Yes, you have to take this because God told me before I left my home I would be giving my cross away. If He is telling me to give this one away, He has one better to give me."* I told her this one had sapphires so maybe He would give me a cross with big diamonds. I laughed and continued, *"You know, maybe it's a big Oprah cross."* Yes, that's what I thought. Why not?

I went on, *"If you do not take this one, I will miss my blessing, so please take it because God wants you to have it."* She finally agreed after saying, *"Are you sure?"* half a dozen times.

I believe with all my heart that for me to receive what God has for me that I must first be obedient—giving away my favorite cross in this instance. It had to be my desire for her to have it. So with a glowing smile on my face, and with no regrets, I freely gave it to her.

You see, God had just proved Himself to me. I did hear Him, and He wanted her to have that cross. She saw the beauty of it saying the words I thought I would never hear. Even more than that, He wanted to see if I had faith in His word!

So you see, faith by itself isn't enough. Unless it produces good deeds, it is dead and useless. James 2:17 | NLT

What are the chances of God telling me that I would give my favorite cross away on the same day that someone stops me and says the words I told God I would have to hear in order to be obedient to His Word. The chances of that happening were slim to none, and yet it did happen! That's why I say, *"It's a God thing!"*

Many years passed after giving my sapphire cross away. I was home alone one day sitting on my couch, thanking and praising God for all he had done for me—for all the things He had given me, times He had talked to me and showed me He was real, all of the miracles I had seen, and so on. I wanted to ask Him something that had been on my mind and bothering me for quite some time now. I thought about all those years back when He wanted me to give my favorite cross away and I knew without any doubt that it was God talking to me—that it had been a divine appointment.

Despite the years that had passed, I still had not received the replacement that I thought I would after giving my favorite cross away. Why wouldn't I think that's what He would do because I truly loved that cross? As I started talking to Him, tears trickled down my cheek. I told Him that I gave away my favorite cross in faith, believing that He would replace it with another one.

*Give and you will receive. Your gift will return
to you in full–pressed down, shaken together
to make room for more, running over, and
poured into your lap. The amount you give will
determine the amount you get back.*
Luke 6:38 | NLT

By this time the tears had turned from a slow trickle to a stream, rolling down my face as my words were completely choked up. As I sat pondering about what I was going to say to God if He told me something I did not want to hear, He suddenly spoke, *"Leisa, every time you sell Ornaments of Grace, I bless you because you gave your favorite cross away. I have given you the ability to design and make your own crosses, and many admire them."*

I heard Him continue, *"Leisa, what did she say to you when standing in front of the church doors, those words you did not want to hear?"* By this time, I was crying uncontrollably because I remembered the words that she said to me. For the first time, I realized they were the same words all my customers tell me they hear while wearing Ornaments of Grace Crosses. I realized that God's ways are not our ways.

I would have settled for one cross, but He gave me the ability to make my own crosses that were even more gorgeous than the sapphire one I gave away. He is a faithful God, and He continues to bless me now after so many years have passed, after I gave away my favorite cross in faith.

"My thoughts are nothing like your thoughts,"
says the Lord. "And My ways are far beyond
anything you could imagine. For just as the
heavens are higher than the earth, so My ways are
higher than your ways and My thoughts higher
than your thoughts." Isaiah 55:8-9 | NLT

CHAPTER 12

Fasting for a Miracle

One evening, my daughter, Chelsi, came to me explaining that her feet hurt when she would stand or walk. She thought there was something under her foot, so I had her sit down to take a look, but I couldn't really see anything.

Chelsi said, *"Mama, it feels like I have BBs in my feet."* I felt her foot again, and it did feel like BBs were in there under the skin. We counted about ten I guess, but I had no idea what it was. I told her they would probably go away and she would be okay. A few more days passed, and she said they were not going away—she had even more. Chelsi sat down on a chair and flipped her foot over, and I started counting. I was astonished and stopped counting at twenty-five.

I took her to our family doctor who said they were a certain kind of wart called plantar warts. They would apparently have to be surgically removed.

Plantar warts are about the size of a pencil eraser. But some grow bigger. Sometimes plantar warts can grow in clusters; those are called mosaic warts. Foot warts are challenging to treat because most of the wart lies below the skin surface. Eventually, in about two years, most warts go away without treatment. Warts can, however, cause irritation or minor pain, depending on their location. Doctors' treatments for plantar warts are generally more effective. They include freezing the wart off with liquid nitrogen, removing the wart with laser or surgery.

I had to remind myself we no longer had health insurance—cha-ching, cha-ching is all I heard in my mind—we did not have the money so surgery was not an option for us.

At the very beginning, I told God that if I quit my job at Walmart to open the gift store that He wanted me to open, He would have to provide. We couldn't have any doctor or hospital bills because we would no longer have health insurance. I decided when I got home that I would pray over Chelsi's foot, and I decided I would fast for seven days—nothing to eat! Believing that God would see my humbled heart and heal her foot, this would be the longest I would fast without anything to eat. I was going to *believe* for a *miracle*, and after seven days the warts would have all disappeared.

Then no one will notice that you are fasting, except your Father, who knows what you do in private. And your Father, who sees everything, will reward you. Matthew 6:18 | NLT

I woke up early on the morning of the eighth day, jumped out of bed, and ran to Chelsi's bedroom. I yanked up the covers from the bottom of the bed and grabbed her foot, expecting to see nothing. But they were still there! I didn't get upset. I still believed God was going to heal her and the warts would disappear all in His timing, not mine.

About five days later, Chelsi ran to the kitchen with excitement in her voice. *"Mama, look at my feet! I've got holes in them, and I can see to pick the warts out."*

I swiftly walked over to Chelsi not fully understanding what she was saying—what do you mean, holes in your foot?! I looked down at the foot in question, and shock soon covered my face. There were holes everywhere! Every wart had formed a hole over it, and the warts had all turned black. We just needed to take a toothpick and pluck them out. After about a week, all of the holes that had appeared, closed completely up. I believed I would receive a miracle after my offering of prayer and fasting by the warts simply disappearing. However, God showed me a true miracle instead—giving me a way to remove the warts, participating in His miracle and seeing exactly how he healed Chelsi.

CHAPTER 13

The Alabaster Box

One summer morning in 2003, while at the store, I realized I needed to order more of the beautiful bottles from Egypt for my poem, *"Tears in a Bottle."* I called Zackary, a vendor, and gave him my order. In our conversation, I mentioned that God had given me a poem for a prayer box as well.

He asked me what box I was using for the poem, as he had alabaster boxes.

I told him that I had jeweled boxes from another company that I was using for the poem, *"The Prayer Box."*

Right then, I heard God say, *"Order one hundred alabaster boxes."*

So I told Zackary I would like to order one hundred of his alabaster boxes, but I had no idea why. I did not need them at the time. I had no poem and no idea why God wanted me to order them.

However, I do know the story mentioned in the Bible about the woman breaking the alabaster box of expensive perfume. She loved Jesus so much she did not care how expensive it was.

When a certain immoral woman from that city heard He was eating there, she brought a beautiful alabaster jar filled with expensive perfume. Then she knelt behind Him at His feet, weeping. Her tears fell on His feet, and she wiped them off with her hair. Then she kept kissing His feet and putting perfume on them.
Luke 7:37-38 | NLT

I got off the phone and said, *"God, now I at least need a poem for the alabaster box."* A few months later, I was sitting under the hair dryer at the beauty shop when God gave me the first three lines of a poem. I asked my cousin, Monica, if she would please bring me a piece of paper and a pen. I wrote the first three lines down, folded up the paper, and put it in the side pocket of my purse.

Five days later, on the way home late at night from Monroe, Louisiana, God gave me more of the poem. When I got home, I sat down at the table and finished the poem *"The Alabaster Box."* The poem was so beautiful I would read it repeatedly.

The next morning as I was driving back to Monroe, I asked God, *"Why the alabaster box? What makes it so important?"*

I heard God say, *"Leisa, you are just like the alabaster box; you have to be broken."* Immediately, I started weeping. I knew what He meant when I heard those words. I had to be a vessel willing to be broken to be a servant of Jesus. I would never have compared the breaking of the alabaster box with the breaking of my flesh—breaking away from all the bad things my flesh fights against daily.

I still felt there was something else, so I asked God, *"Why me? What did I do to deserve this?"*

I then heard God say, *"Leisa, what did you do thirty-nine days ago?"*

Are you serious?!? I can hardly remember what I did yesterday and He wanted me to think back over a month previous. However, in obedience, I tried to figure out where I was and what I was doing. I finally remembered that I was in Houston, Texas with some ladies from my church at the *"Woman Thou Art Loosed"* conference by Bishop T.D. Jakes.

God asked me, *"Do you remember what you did?"*

I replied, *"I remember."*

It was the day before our church was to leave for home as we were at the end of the conference. T.D. Jakes had said that there were one hundred women who were supposed to give one thousand dollars. I was sitting there crying because

I wished I had it to give. The ushers were handing out the envelopes for our giving, and I started filling mine out. I looked in my purse to see how much money I had left. I still had to eat supper and then breakfast the next morning, plus have a little extra for the eight-hour trip back home. After I put my money in the envelope, I closed it up. I then heard God say to me, *"Give all you have."*

"God, I will not have any money left for food or anything!"

God then told me, *"You can fast until you get home."*

I replied, *"Okay, I can do that."*

However, I was wondering why God would want me to do this. I got another envelope, filled it out, and put all the money I had in it. I was still crying, and my heart was hurting because I wanted to give the thousand dollars that I did not have.

I then heard God say, *"Leisa, you wanted to give what you did not have, but when you gave ALL you had, I saw your heart. When you gave all you had, you gave more than the ones that gave a thousand."*

I then said, *"God, I remembered the story about the widow woman in the Bible."*

Jesus sat down near the collection box in the Temple and watched as the crowds dropped in their money. Many rich people put in large amounts. Then a poor widow came and dropped

in two small coins. Jesus called His disciples to
Him and said, "I tell you the truth, this poor
widow has given more than all the others who are
making contributions. For they gave a tiny part
of their surplus, but she, poor as she is, has given
everything she had to live on."
Mark 12:41-44 | NLT

Let us not forget the temptation the devil puts on us as soon as we start doing something to honor God. As I was fasting on our return trip from the conference, everyone wanted to stop and eat.

As the bus stopped at McDonald's, everyone stepped off to eat except for me. However, it was summer and hot so I decided to go in where it was nice and cool. I opened the doors to McDonald's when all of a sudden the overwhelming aroma of food cooking hit me. Yes, I could literally smell everything they were cooking! I was so hungry, and I wanted to eat, but I knew I could not. I had friends asking me why I was not going to eat, and a few even offered to buy my food.

If roles were reversed, I would have thought the same thing—that the one person not eating had no money. I could not let them know I was fasting, so I just smiled and thanked them for offering to buy my lunch, but I was fine.

And when you fast, don't make it obvious, as the
hypocrites do, for they try to look miserable and

disheveled so people will admire them for their
fasting. I tell you the truth, that is the only reward
they will ever get. But when you fast, comb your
hair and wash your face. Then no one will notice
that you are fasting, except your Father, who
knows what you do in private. And your Father,
who sees everything, will reward you.
Matthew 6:16-18 | NLT

In the end, I made it home. I believe when I gave all I had, it brought forth my blessing for the alabaster box.

The next day, I had an idea; I would order anointing oil straight from Jerusalem for the alabaster box. I did not pray about this portion of the box as I really thought this was a perfect complement to the box. Why pray about it? The woman mentioned in the Bible had perfume in her box, and I would have anointing oil in mine.

To me, it could not get any better than ordering anointing oil from Jerusalem. Wow! I thought, *This is going to be awesome.*

So I ordered four big bottles, and then I transferred the anointing oil to glass vials for the alabaster boxes. I was to speak at our Ladies' Ministry Meeting in September, and I wanted to give away my first one—not sell it.

Zackary sent me two boxes by three-day air. Those were the only ones he had on hand because the rest of my order was being shipped from Egypt. I know you are wondering why Egypt? Well, this was what I found out after researching the alabaster box mentioned in the Bible:

According to Easton's Bible Dictionary: alabaster occurs only in the New Testament in connection with the box of "ointment of very precious spikenard." These boxes were made from a stone found near Alabastron in Egypt, and from this circumstance the Greeks gave them the name of the city where they were made. The name was then given to the stone of which they were made; and finally to all perfume vessels, of whatever material they were formed. This stone resembles marble, but is softer in its texture, and hence very easily wrought into boxes.

I got the boxes in the day before I was to speak at the meeting. One of the boxes was really too big so I was going to carry it home as a gift to myself. When suddenly, I heard God say, *"No, you are not. You are going to break that alabaster box and give every person there a piece of the box."* I thought that was a great idea because everyone would leave with a piece of the box since I only had one to give away. That was obviously God's plan all along.

I was now searching for my hammer, and something to keep the alabaster box from flying across the store once I hit it. I knew I would have to continue to break the box to have plenty of pieces so everybody would get one.

I decided to use paper towels,and lay the box upside down on a double piece, covering the top part also with a double piece as well. I did not want stray shards to break off and fly across the store hitting something. I took my hammer, pulled back my arm, and down the hammer came. Bam! I pulled back the paper towel expecting to see at least two pieces, but the box had not broken. I did it again with a little more force, and again nothing happened. Every time I pulled back that paper towel to see if it was broken, I got frustrated because it simply would not break. With all the strength I had, I hit it again, and still nothing.

I said, *"God, this box does not want to break."*

He replied, *"Yes, just like your flesh, it does not want to be broken."*

It was as if he was using me and the alabaster box to make a very important statement. Our flesh loves sin and does not want to be broken. God cannot use us as a servant until we have been broken. It is our choice; He will not break us unless we are willing. I am not going to lie, it hurts to be broken. But it has to be our desire—and then He will use us. I finally broke the box into many pieces after God made His point about being broken.

In a wealthy home some utensils are made of gold and silver, and some are made of wood and clay. The expensive utensils are used for special

occasions, and the cheap ones are for everyday
use. If you keep yourself pure, you will be a
special utensil for honorable use. Your life will be
clean, and you will be ready for the Master to use
you for every good work.
2 Timothy 2:20-21 | NLT

With the boxes and oils in place, it was time to design the tag. God told me the artwork on the top of the tag needed to be vines and grapes.

I said, *"God, shouldn't this be an olive tree? That's what the anointing oil is made from, the olive trees in Galilee and Jerusalem."*

Still not understanding, but wanting to be obedient, I had the vines and the grapes designed for the top of the card. The following Sunday, I was sitting in church when God said, *"Leisa, the anointing oil you ordered to go in the alabaster box was not what I wanted."*

I said, *"God, you cannot get any better than this. I've got the best."*

"It is not what I wanted," said God.

I tried to figure out what other anointing oil would be better than what I had ordered. The following Monday, I got on the internet and started searching for spikenard because that is what the woman in the Bible had. Every time I found spikenard, it was too expensive.

I said, *"God, nobody will be able to buy the alabaster box with spikenard. It will be too expensive. What's the use?"*

Then I came across a website that said *"Essential Oil Specialist"* and I felt in my spirit that I was supposed to call this company. I did not know why at first, maybe it was just to ask how much their spikenard was. The person who answered the phone that day asked me what I was going to do with spikenard.

I replied, *"I'm going to use it for anointing oil. God gave me a poem called "The Alabaster Box" and the oil will be placed inside the box in a glass vial."*

The essential oils lady said, *"You cannot put one-hundred percent pure spikenard on your skin. You have to have a carrier oil to mix it with. It only takes a little spikenard."*

Then I asked, *"What does this spikenard smell like?"*

She then replied, *"It's an earthy scent that doesn't smell too good."*

I thought, *"God, I do not know where you are going with this, but who would want to put on stinky anointing oil?"*

The lady then interjected, *"Why don't I try to make you your own blend of anointing oil?"* A light bulb came on. *Okay, God. I kind of see where you are going, but I still don't know what you are doing,* I thought.

When I got off the phone after speaking with the specialist, I immediately prayed saying, *"God, I still don't know what*

you are doing, and I do not know where you are going, but this
I do know, that phone call was a divine appointment. I know
the person that I spoke to on the other end of the telephone was
a believer in you, God. I am asking that you give her the blend;
you give her the formula that you intend to go in this alabaster
box. God, I know that there is a reason behind this and I do not
know what it is yet, but I will."

She emailed me the formula and told me what blend to write on a card. By now I should have known that this is the blend that God wanted, but No! He knew He would have to confirm it to me before I would believe this is what He wanted in the alabaster box.

Remember the artwork on the card of the vines and grapes? The carrier oil that the specialist put in the special blend of anointing oil was not olive oil; it was grapeseed oil. Wow, What a sign!

This special, formulated anointing oil was to be in remembrance of our Lord and Savior, Jesus Christ. Here is what went on the card, including the special blend's ingredients:

"In Remembrance of Me"
Luke 22:19

"SPIKENARD"

The woman mentioned in the Bible anointed Jesus with Spikenard.

This prepares Him for burial, and is to remind us He died for all!

But thank God! He has made us His captives and continues to lead us along in Christ's triumphal procession. Now He uses us to spread the knowledge of Christ everywhere, like a sweet perfume. Our lives are a Christ-like fragrance rising up to God. But this fragrance is perceived differently by those who are being saved and by those who are perishing.
2 Corinthians 2:14-15 | NLT

"CORIANDER"

Manna, the Hebrew name given by the Israelites, meant, *"What is it?"* Coriander is an herb that grows to be 2 to 3 ft. tall. The plant produces seed, which is used for flavoring food even to this day. A sample of *"The Bread"* was commanded to be kept to show to future generations of the provision of God in the wilderness. This sample was more than a keepsake; it was a sign of the Covenant. Manna nurtured the people and gave life for 40 years. As such, it was a type of Christ.

The Israelites called the food manna. It was white like coriander seed, and it tasted like honey wafers.

Then Moses said, "This is what the Lord has commanded: Fill a two-quart container with

manna to preserve it for your descendants. Then
later generations will be able to see the food I
gave you in the wilderness when I set you free
from Egypt."
Moses said to Aaron, "Get a jar and fill it with
two quarts of manna. Then put it in a sacred
place before the Lord to preserve it for all future
generations."
Aaron did just as the Lord had commanded
Moses.
He eventually placed it in the Ark of the
Covenant-in front of the stone tablets inscribed
with the terms of the covenant.
Exodus 16:31-34 | NLT

A direct correlation can be seen every time the Eucharist is observed and the one officiating repeats Christ's words. The wine of the Lord's Supper depicts the giving of life, a sacrifice of blood, which inaugurates the New Covenant for those who respond to Jesus' offer of salvation. Jesus died on the cross in our place and for our sins.

He took some bread and gave thanks to God for
it. Then He broke it in pieces and gave it to the
disciples, saying, "This is My body, which is given
for you. Do this to remember Me."
After supper He took another cup of wine and
said, "This cup is the new covenant between God

and His people–an agreement confirmed with My
blood, which is poured out as a sacrifice for you.
Luke 22:19-20 | NLT

"CEDAR WOOD"

A strong sort of wood, sweet, durable, and therefore will never rot, typifying the firmness and continuance of the church. The galleries for walking are of fir. Wood was pleasing both to the sight and to the smell, intimating the delight, which the saints take in walking with Christ.

fragrant cedar branches are the beams of
our house,
and pleasant smelling firs are the rafters
Song of Solomon 1:17 | NLT

"ROSE"

To remind us of beauty and fragrance, to express His presence with His people in this world, the easiness of their access to Him, and the beauty and sweetness which they find in Him.

I am the rose of Sharon,
Song of Solomon 2:1 | NLT

"GRAPES" (GRAPE SEED OIL)

The first Miracle recorded in the New Testament was when Jesus turned water into wine.

This miraculous sign at Cana in Galilee was the
first time Jesus revealed His glory.
And His disciples believed in Him.
John 2:11 | NLT

"I am the true grapevine,"
John 15:1 | NLT

THE ALABASTER BOX

This is a box that's a special kind.
It's holding something precious, that will take you back
in time.
There she stood behind him, with it broken and in her hand.
No matter what the cost, anointing the Master was her plan.
To her knees she fell, with tears that washed his feet.
Wiping them with her hair and a Kiss that was complete.
So anoint them in his name, and call out to the Master.
When you take this precious oil, from this box of alabaster.
© Leisa Spann

This is the card god had me design for the alabaster box.

CHAPTER 14

A Rose in Loving Memory

When God first started giving me poetry, He would typically wake me up between 2:00 and 3:00 a.m. On one particular morning, God woke me up, and I knew He was going to give me a poem.

I grabbed a notebook and pen, and off to the living room I went. I sat there waiting; I knew the poem was about a rose. He gave me a few lines, but it wasn't coming very quickly. God doesn't give me poems in the same way He talks to me— it's more of a slow and painful process. It's like He wants me to fill in the blanks. I was very tired, so I said, *"God, no one is going to buy a poem about a rose. I'm really sleepy and going back to bed."*

The next morning, I thought about the poem, but I could only remember it was about a rose. That's it. Months passed without a thought on the subject.

One day, I heard my store's bell go off, and a lady walked in. I said, *"Welcome to Just a Touch of Heaven. If there's anything I can help you with, just let me know."* The lady said she wasn't from Oak Grove. She was just passing through. She walked around the store browsing and looking at what I had to sell when she saw the cross hanging behind the counter.

"Wow!" she said. *"That cross is just beautiful. Wherever did you find that?"* That was my cue to share my testimony about the cross. When I finished the testimony, she said, *"Let me share a testimony with you."*

She continued, *"One morning, many years ago, my son came to me and asked to borrow my credit card so he could buy his girlfriend a dozen roses. I grabbed my purse, pulled out my credit card and handed it to him, and out the door he went. As he left, I began thinking, 'Here I am buying someone a dozen roses when I've never had anyone give me a dozen roses.' I started feeling sorry for myself, and I asked God, 'Am I not worthy enough for a dozen roses?' I then had to leave the house to pay a few bills."*

The lady went on, *"As I was driving, I heard God tell me to go to a particular water company and walk inside. A quick reply to God was, 'What am I supposed to do there? That's not where I pay my water bill. God, that's crazy.' I heard him again* tell me to stop and go inside. I was still driving at this point because I was trying to figure out why in the world He would have me go there. Again, for the third time, He told me the same thing. I finally decided to stop and go in, not knowing what I would do or say once I stepped through the door. When I walked in, I saw two ladies arguing with each other."

"I heard one say, 'I'm not taking them home, you can take them home with you.' Then the other, 'No, I'm not taking them home either because my husband will assume I'm having an affair.'"

"I then stepped in not knowing what they were arguing about and said, 'I'll take them.'"

"They both turned their head and looked at me and said, 'You will?'"

"I then replied, 'Yes, I will. What am I taking home?'"

"One of the ladies said, 'We helped out a nice gentleman earlier with a problem, and he sent us a dozen beautiful roses. Both of us are married, and we don't want to leave them here over the weekend because they will wilt and die. We don't want either of our husbands to think we are having an affair, so it's great that you will take them home with you.'"

"I then heard God say to me, 'You are worthy of a dozen roses.'"

"Wow," I said, "Who can say God sent them a dozen roses?"

After recounting this story, the lady in my store then looked at me and said, *"Have you ever written a poem about a rose?"* Oh, my gosh! I burst into tears. Was she kidding me? Did she just say that to me?

In that exact moment, I felt God sent this woman into my store to tell me that story because I had turned my back on Him. I thought I knew what I needed, and I didn't want to write His poem.

After she left my store, I asked God to give me a second chance with the poem. Years passed and no poem came, but every time I thought about a rose, I asked God to forgive me and to please give me another chance.

About five years later, after the encounter with the *"rose lady,"* my phone rang at 5:00 a.m. on Friday, November 9, 2007. Before I answered, a sudden feeling of fear came over me because my phone just doesn't normally ring that early. I felt something was wrong.

I answered, and my brother-in-law's voice was on the other end of the phone saying, *"Leisa, there's been an accident. Clay has died in a wreck."* Clay was my nephew, my sister Cindy's son. He was 19 years old. I got up and went to my daughter's room to wake her with the devastating news.

God blesses those who mourn, for they will be comforted. Matthew 5:4 | NLT

Later on and about mid-morning, my doorbell rang at home. I opened the front door and found a dozen roses. That's right. Chelsi's boyfriend had bought me a dozen roses because of the loss of my nephew. Who buys a dozen roses as a condolence? I had never heard of that before. However, when I opened the door and saw those roses, I knew God was going to give me a poem about a rose. I was so confident it was time.

I told Chelsi's boyfriend the story about what had happened years ago with the roses. Saturday evening, on my way home from the funeral home, God started giving me the poem. He gave me the title first, and then the poem came. This time, God gave me the poem faster than all my others. I pulled over on the side of the road looking for some form of paper to write on. I found a piece of mail and turned it over, using the back side to write the poem on.

I wrote about half of the poem before continuing home. When I got home, I sat down and finished the poem. I sat there in awe of what God had just given me.

Not only did God give me a beautiful poem for Clay, but He provided the rose. I typed the poem on cardstock, printed it, and cut it with scalloped edging. I tied a ribbon to the poem and the rose. The day of Clay's funeral, the rose was put with him and this poem attached.

A ROSE IN LOVING MEMORY

A rose in loving memory that's written on the heart,
to show my love will never part.
The thorns are the pain that I carry inside,
like the dew drops on a rose from the tears I've cried.
The petals feel like velvet soft to the touch,
the memories are what I'll treasure so much.
One day the rose will bloom again,
when we see each other in Heaven, Amen...
©Leisa Spann

It shall blossom abundantly, and rejoice even with joy and singing. Isaiah 35:2 | NLT

CHAPTER 15

The Stranger

One hot summer day, while at the store, I heard the doorbell ring. It was an elderly woman accompanied by a younger woman. I felt they were mother and daughter and said to them, *"If I can help you with anything, just let me know."*

The elderly woman spoke up and said, *"We are just looking."*

After about fifteen minutes or so they were still there looking around the store when the elderly woman said, *"That Cross is beautiful!"* Well, that was my cue. I told them the whole story, and the elderly woman said, *"Will you pray for my husband? He's having problems with his leg, and they are talking about amputation."*

That's when I heard God say to me, *"Leisa, tell her to bring him in. And you anoint him and pray for his healing."*

Then Jesus told them, "I tell you the truth, if you have faith and don't doubt, you can do things like this and much more. You can pray for anything, and if you have faith, you will receive it."
Matthew 21:21-22 | NLT

I then asked the elderly woman, *"Do you think he would let you pick him up and bring him here so I can anoint and pray for him?"*

She then replied, *"I'll go get him. He's in the car!"*

Oh, my gosh! What?! I thought to myself, *They have been in the store for at least thirty minutes, and he's been sitting in the car the whole time.*

She stated, *"He's been in the hospital with his leg, and they were going to amputate it when the doctor came in this morning and told him he had changed his mind. He told him he was going to send him home with some pain pills, and if the pain was unbearable and he couldn't stand it anymore to come back and they would amputate. We are waiting on the prescription to be filled at Walmart."*

Wow, you could have knocked me down with a feather!

I had no idea he was in the car, but God did. I said, *"Go get him!"* I knew God was going to heal this man who was a stranger to me. They left to go get him, and while they were gone, I moved a chair to the front of the store so he wouldn't have very far to walk. I also grabbed my anointing oil.

They were coming back in the store with him; they each had him by the arm on both of his sides and moved at a very slow pace because of his leg. To top it off, he had a big, black, bulky boot on his leg.

This was the first time I saw this type of boot. The ladies eventually brought him safely to the chair, and I introduced myself.

I said, *"Hello, my name is Leisa, and I'm a servant for the Lord. I would like to anoint and pray for you to be healed. I believe God can heal you. However, do you believe God can heal you?"*

He said, *"Yes, I Believe!"*

I then asked, *"Where did this start?"*

He replied, *"It started in my little toe."*

I looked down at his feet, and I couldn't see anything because he had a black sock on. Suddenly, I received a vision of his leg being discolored. And so I asked him, *"Is your leg black and purple?"*

He replied, *"Yes."*

I then took my finger and dipped it in the anointing oil, placing my finger where I thought his little toe was by rubbing the oil on top of his sock. I said to everyone there, *"Let's all hold hands and bow our heads."*

I started praying, believing with every word I spoke that God was listening. It was God who told me to bring this man in for prayer, so I had to believe this was God's will for the stranger to be healed. I prayed for the blood to start flowing from the small toe, where it started from, to the other toes, and then to the foot, the ankle, and the calf of his leg, then to his knee, and finally to his thigh. I prayed for the color to come back alive, healthy and renewed.

When I finished praying, there wasn't a dry eye in the room. You see, I used to think praying with big words and having long prayers is what God wanted, but I simply don't know how to pray like that. I finally figured out it's not the big words and the long prayers God hears, it's the heart!

Search me, O God, and know my heart.
Psalms 139:23 | NLT

The group was at the front door ready to go when the stranger turned around and said to me, *"Thank You!"*

I replied, *"You're thanking the wrong person! I just prayed for you. You need to thank God and let others know He healed you. The blood will start to flow, and you will see the color start to come back."*

He said, *"I will."* They left. And about ten minutes after, I realized I didn't get his name.

Now what, I thought. I'll tell you what, I didn't know this stranger, but I fasted for God to heal him. I believe God saw his faith and knew my heart and with both, he would get his miracle.

A couple of weeks passed by, and I was at Walmart at the service desk talking with a friend when I looked up and saw the stranger's wife come in. She noticed me and came over to where I was standing and said, *"My husband has already been to two different doctors, and both doctors say he now has full circulation in his leg, and the color has come back also."*

Well, I'm sure not ashamed of what my Jesus can do, and so I yelled, *"Hallelujah, Thank You Jesus!"* And with that I did a skip-a-dee-doo-dah right out the door of Walmart. I was so thankful that God sent her in at the same time I was there at Walmart to hear that awesome report!

A few weeks later, I was at the store when the doorbell rang, and I looked up to see my stranger standing there. He said, *"I just wanted to come by and again thank you and to tell you I went to church today at a men's ministry meeting and stood up and gave my testimony of God healing my leg from amputation."* I thanked him for coming in to see me and letting me know how that blesses my heart.

I can't explain why God heals some and not others. We have to put our trust in Him and know that His power and wisdom is greater than ours.

CHAPTER 16

A Storm is Coming

One day during 2005, a hurricane was making its way through Louisiana. In preparation, I went to Walmart to stock up on gallons of water and a few groceries to get us by just in case the electricity went out.

Our home is run completely on electricity and we are limited in what we can do as far as cooking because of this. So to stock up, we have to buy food we don't have to cook or put in the refrigerator. The hurricane was a Category 4 and had already hit down south across the southern states of Louisiana and Mississippi and was now moving its way north.

We live in the northeast corner of Louisiana, about twenty miles from the Arkansas line and about three hundred fifty miles from the bottom of south Louisiana. Even though this particular hurricane had weakened some, there was still a chance of tornadoes forming, along with heavy rain and winds. At that point, the hurricane is no longer a hurricane but can still pack quite a punch by the time it gets to where we live. This particular hurricane was slated to hit our area of the state on this certain night.

When I drove up onto our driveway, I heard God say, *"Do NOT park all the way up to the basketball goal. It's going to fall tonight!"* So I parked in the middle of our driveway.

Joyful are those who listen to me.
Proverbs 8:34 | NLT

It did look odd parking that way because it left little room for anyone else to park behind me. I was unloading the groceries in the kitchen when I heard my husband come in with keys jiggling. I knew that sound was the jingle of my keys, so I made my way into the living room where he was standing to see what he was doing with my keys.

He handed me my keys and said, *"I moved your SUV up. Why did you park that far back?"*

I replied, *"God told me the basketball goal is going to fall tonight."*

He laughed and said, *"Leisa, we have had that basketball goal for years and have been through many storms, and it has not budged one inch!"*

Well, that left a bad taste in my mouth, as this disbelief really rubbed me the wrong way. I felt he didn't believe what I had told him. In addition, we were discussing the fate of a brand new SUV I had just purchased a few weeks prior. I had not even made my first note yet.

I let my husband talk me out of a warning God gave me. Yes, I could have stood firm in my faith and took my keys and put the SUV back where I had parked it earlier. But I didn't. How many times have we each let someone talk us out of something we believe because he or she didn't believe it themselves? We start to second guess ourselves and eventually make the wrong decision.

I started to think, *Well, he's right. We have had that basketball goal for years, and it has not moved an inch.* So I let him talk me out of it, not listening to God's warning about the basketball goal falling.

I finally said to Gary, *"If that basketball goal falls on my SUV tonight, you are going into the storm to remove it!"*

He laughed and said, *"Okay!"*

I'm very fearful of storms, and I tell myself all the time that God has not given me this fear.

God has not given us a spirit of fear and timidity, but of power, love, and self-discipline.
2 Timothy 1:7 | NLT

It was time for bed so I turned on the porch light to see what was to come with the storm. We went to bed around 10:00 p.m., and I was in a deep sleep until about 11:30 p.m. when I heard a loud BOOM. I was still dazed and half asleep when I woke up. I didn't know what was going on. Was it a tornado? I could hear the wind howling and fear had now consumed me.

I wanted to go look out the window, but I thought, *What if the window breaks while I'm in front of it?!?* All of these emotions flooded my brain while Gary kept snoring away! *How could he sleep through this?*

I decided to jump up and run to our bedroom window to see if I could see anything. I had to find out what the thud was. I used my fingers to open a spot in the blinds. It was raining so hard. As I glanced to the right side where the trees were, I saw nothing. Then I looked to the left side of the house and screamed with horror. There was my SUV with the basketball goal on top of the hood!

I yelled at Gary, who was now awake, and said, *"The basketball goal is on the hood of my SUV. Go get it off."* His face showed it all—he was STUNNED! He got up and went into the storm and pulled it off my SUV.

God warned me the basketball goal was going to fall, and I let my husband talk me out of it. And now I was not only mad at him for talking me out of it with his reasoning and laughing, but I was also mad at myself because I didn't stand firm in my own faith!

I have a great relationship with God, and that's what He wants from each of us. He wants a relationship. God doesn't care what denomination we are. He wants a one-on-one relationship with us, individually.

> *My dear brothers and sisters, be strong and immovable. Always work enthusiastically for the Lord, for you know that nothing you do for the Lord is ever useless.*
> *1 Corinthians 15:58 | NLT*

CHAPTER 17

He Washed Me White As Snow

One spring morning, my business phone rang at my home. I noticed the call was coming from Arkansas and I answered the phone as always, saying, *"Just a Touch of Heaven, this is Leisa, can I help you?"*

A voice on the other end said, *"Yes, I sure hope so."*

She continued, *"My name is V, short for Vivian, and I saw someone wearing one of the beautiful crosses that you designed and made. That cross was the most beautiful cross I have ever seen, and I have to have one. The Crown of Glory is the one I would buy, I think."*

I told her she could order online through my website or by phone.

V responded, *"Oh no, honey. I want to come pick it up."*

"I do not have a walk-in store anymore," I replied.

She then said, *"Oh, please, let me come to your home. I need one of your crosses, and I want to see them all."* She sounded so desperate as she pleaded her case.

I finally said, *"Okay, just this one time."*

She planned to come the next day, and as we were talking, V told me about her ministry centered on salvation from a uniquely different perspective. The ministry was based on the metamorphosis of the caterpillar, as it eventually turns into a beautiful butterfly. When we accept Jesus as our Lord and Savior, we too become new creatures—just like the caterpillar.

This means that anyone who belongs to Christ has become a new person. The old life is gone; a new life has begun!
2 Corinthians 5:17 | NLT

V continued, *"I'm called the butterfly lady because of my ministry."* It was about that time that I heard God say to me, *"Make her a butterfly cross and give it to her tomorrow."* I did not tell her anything about what God had just said; it was to be a surprise for her.

I got off the phone and went to work on her butterfly cross so it would be ready to go the next day. When she arrived, I had all my Ornaments of Grace crosses, plus the butterfly cross I had made for her on display and all lined up for her to easily view.

When she came in, she was so overwhelmed by the options that she didn't know which one she wanted, even though she had stated the day before it was the Crown of Glory she was interested in. She was making her way down the line, looking at all the detail in each cross, when her eyes spotted the butterfly cross.

"Oh, no!" she said, "I came after the Crown of Glory, and now I see this one! How can I make my mind up now?"

Well, I finally decided to tell her that the butterfly cross was a gift to her from God, and He had told me to make it yesterday when we were on the phone talking. Tears started streaming down her face uncontrollably.

"Oh!" she said, "I could never repay you for a gift like this."

I then explained to her, "You owe me nothing, and the request was from God to make you this cross. He will bless me one day for my obedience, and you are not to worry about it."

By this time, we both stood there crying. I knew God was there too, as I could feel the Holy Spirit all around us. The gift was humbling to V; I could see it. She kept asking me how I make and create such beautiful crosses. My simple reply was, *"It's a God thing!"*

V was just another friend that God ordained to cross my path. We all have seasons in our lives when God sends someone along to bless us or to be a stepping stone, helping us to accomplish all that He sets before us. Perhaps you are wondering how V was one of those blessings to me. Let me explain.

As our friendship grew, V showed her crosses to everyone she came across, and within a year, she had bought even more for herself. After about a year and a half, V called me to ask if I would sell my crosses at a home show in Arkansas at her daughter-in-law's house, as she had friends and family who wanted to purchase some crosses.

The day came for me to travel to Arkansas for the home show. I wanted to get there with plenty of time to get everything set up and displayed before people started arriving. I was so excited to see V when she showed up, and she had not come empty-handed. She said, *"I made something for you,"* as she handed me a beautiful, round, crocheted box.

"Open it," she said.

I opened the box, and what I saw was simply amazing! V had made me paper snowflakes. Every snowflake was different; no one snowflake looked like another. I told her that I had never seen anything like that before.

V said, *"I made those for you to put on your Christmas tree this year."*

I looked at her and replied, *"How in the world did you make these?"*

How ironic was it that I asked her the same question that she had asked me about a year and a half before when she inquired about my crosses?

Making my crosses was easy for me. However, when I looked at what V made, I thought, *"Wow, how did V do that?"* God gives all of us gifts. My gifts were designing and making jewelry and writing poetry. V had a gift of making snowflakes out of paper. You see, there was a poem God wanted to give me, but first I had some seed planting to do. When I was obedient and made a butterfly cross for someone I had never met, someone I didn't even know, it was then that my faith in God's Word could bring forth my blessing.

We will all give to people we know—family and friends. However, to give a gift to someone you just talked to on the phone is truly giving from your heart. Yes, I was obedient when I made the butterfly cross for her, and I knew God would bless me for that somehow, I just didn't know how. So the day I opened up the box, I said to V, *"Maybe God will give me a poem about a snowflake."*

A few months later, in November, the weather station predicted snow. In Louisiana, we do not see much snow; we still run our air conditioners in November. We may get sleet or ice in January or February, but not snow.

I went to my front door and opened it up, awestruck by what I saw. Snow was falling. It was beautiful and thick. I saw big flakes and small flakes. And I felt the Holy Spirit all around me. It was like God had put magnifying glasses on my eyes that morning because he wanted me to see the beauty of the snowflakes. I just knew God was going to give me a poem about a snowflake. I shut my front door, grabbed my notebook, sat down on my couch, and wrote the poem *"Legend of the Snowflake."*

LEGEND OF THE SNOWFLAKE

This is the legend of the snowflake,
it's like no other kind.
Each one is very special and unique in its design.
They fall from the angels' wings,
as they dance before the Lord.
Singing praises to the King, all in one accord.
It's the beauty of the snowflake,
a reminder from up above.
That I've been washed as white as snow,
all because of LOVE.
© *Leisa Spann*

Purify me from my sins, and I will be clean; wash me, and I will be whiter than snow.
Psalms 51:7 | NLT

CHAPTER 18

The Fleur-de-Lis

One cool spring morning in 2006, my phone rang. It was Gail, my product rep, in Louisiana. Gail would travel from store to store in North Louisiana representing my product line, taking orders for me. At the time, I had my framed poetry and my newly-designed belt buckles. This particular morning she called and said, *"I have a customer who saw the new belt buckles. The customer loved the cross buckles and said they were beautiful, but she would love to have one with the fleur-de-lis."*

My reply was, *"Is that the emblem on the New Orleans Saints' helmet?"*

Gail laughed at me and said, *"Yes."*

I felt really stupid not knowing the name of the emblem, even though it's widely used in Louisiana, and I've lived here practically my whole life. I explained to Gail that I only use crosses to make my buckles because of what the cross represents, and I didn't know the history of that emblem.

I said, *"Gail, I will do some research and let you know. However, I must know that it's a God thing before I will make it."*

Praising God to make Him happy is rewarding for me. I believe when God sees my heart, He knows that I'm not doing it for monetary gain; it glorifies Him.

Seek the Kingdom of God above all else, and live righteously, and He will give you everything you need. Matthew 6:33 | NLT

When I got off the phone, I called Pam, a store owner in Natchitoches, Louisiana who carried my framed poetry at the time. When she answered, I told her I needed to learn how to pronounce and spell the name of the emblem that's on the New Orleans Saints' helmet. Well, I felt as if it was *"Laugh-at-Leisa Day"* because she thought it was funny too.

Over the phone, Pam taught me how to pronounce fleur-de-lis and told me how to spell it. When I got off the phone, I prayed and asked God for His guidance before doing an online search of the emblem's meaning. If He wanted me to do the buckle with the fleur-de-lis design on it, He needed to give me a sign.

For about forty-five minutes I searched and read what was on the internet just by keying in the word *"fleur-de-lis."* What I found was overwhelming. I had no idea it was considered a Christian symbol and has been around for thousands of years. Let me clarify that it may have not started out as a Christian symbol. However, the cross wasn't a Christian symbol either until Jesus was crucified on one.

The fleur-de-lis symbol has been regarded as a sign of purity ever since antiquity. The Roman Catholic Church adopted it to represent the Virgin Mary. The Fleur was considered the lily flower and symbolized the Holy Trinity. The more I read, the more I knew *"It's a God Thing!"*

Just about the time that I decided I didn't need a sign, God gave me one anyway, and boy was it a sign! When I scrolled down a little further on the page, I saw in big, black, bold letters *"WOODWARD ON THE FLEUR-DE-LIS!"* I burst into tears; my hair on the back of my neck stood straight up. I didn't know what that really meant, but Woodward was my birth name. You see, I was adopted. The man who adopted me was my mom's second husband.

Deep down inside, I never wanted to be adopted. I didn't get to see my real dad very much, maybe twice a year because he worked overseas on a big boat. The few times a year I did get to see him left me waving good-bye in his rearview mirror, crying and wondering when I would see him again. I've always had a loving relationship with my real dad, Jerry, so when I saw *"Woodward,"* God knew that was all the sign I needed. However, He was not finished with me yet. Even though I had received the sign needed to make the buckle for the customer, He wanted to give me even more.

That night, I sat down with my notebook in hand, and God gave me this beautiful poem. It now brings meaning to the fleur-de-lis.

FLEUR-DE-LIS

"The Flower of the Lily"
This is the Fleur-de-Lis, it's a legend of a special kind.
It's called the golden lily that will take you back in time.
It's said that lilies sprung up, from the tears shed by Eve.
Leaving Eden behind that day, her broken heart did grieve.
It symbolized purity upon Christians back then.
For life, faith and wisdom, the old was new again.
It represents the Trinity the petals that you see.
The Father, Son, and Holy Spirit these are the three.
At the foot of the Cross grown by Virgin Mary years ago,
a field of Golden Lilies where her tears made them grow.
© Leisa Spann

Consider the lilies how they grow.
Luke 12:27 | NLT??

CHAPTER 19

Obedience is Better than Sacrifice

Blessings will always follow our obedience to God if we set aside our will and desires for His will and desires.

> *What is more pleasing to the Lord: your burnt offerings and sacrifices or your obedience to His voice? Listen! Obedience is better than sacrifice, and submission is better than offering the fat of rams. 1 Samuel 15:22 | NLT*

I decided to participate in the Christmas City USA Gift Show in Biloxi, Mississippi. This is a huge gift show where over ten thousand shoppers attend in just one weekend. I was taking my Fleur-of-Faith T-shirts as well as my designed jewelry and framed poetry to sell at the show.

Because I had over 300 T-shirts to fold by styles and sizes for the show, I called Mrs. Wilhelmina to help me. We finished in the early evening after folding pretty much all day. All I had left to do was to load them in the cargo trailer before leaving for Biloxi. I paid Mrs. Wilhelmina, hugged her, and thanked her for helping me, as I could not have done it without her.

She exited the door and got in her small truck to leave. On this particular day, she decided not to back out of the driveway, but instead to pull up and try to turn around on the side lot. I didn't know this is what she was doing or I would have warned her about the metal rod sticking out of the ground (the previous owners had put it there to indicate the property line).

Suddenly, I heard a big BOOM! Running outside, I saw the tire had completely blown out—she had run over the rod! This rod was not small; it was about 2 to 3 inches wide, sticking out of the ground about two inches.

As soon as I realized what she had done, I heard God say, *"Tell her you will buy her a new tire."* I paused, thinking this was not my fault, but I knew that it was God's voice I heard. I also knew I would receive a blessing for buying her a new tire. My thought at the time was that God would bless me in sales at the show if I did this. I was not thinking about the obedience part, only the giving part.

I apologized and told Mrs. Wilhelmina that I would buy her a new tire. She said, "*You will do no such thing. This was my fault.*" I informed her that God told me to pay for a new tire and if she didn't let me buy it then I would not be able to receive my blessing. Who could argue with that logic? She conceded.

Thursday morning came and I was on my way to Biloxi with a ten-foot cargo trailer loaded from top to bottom and side to side, weighing about four thousand pounds. After five hours of driving, I arrived at the Coliseum in Biloxi.

As I drove up to one of the side doors, a man motioned for me to go through. Yes, I drove right into the Coliseum and up to my booth. I loved that part. This show is the only one I have participated in that lets you drive up to your booth site. They even have workers to help you unload. Amazing! Once I pulled up to my spot, I went to unlock the trailer's cargo doors.

One of the workers said to me, "*Oh, my. What happened to your tire?*"

I replied, "*What do you mean?*"

"*What did you run over?*" he replied.

I was thoroughly confused at that point, so I walked around the trailer to where he was standing, and my eyes could not believe what I was seeing. I knew immediately at the sight of that tire that my blessing was not going to come to me the way I thought.

The Word of God says that His ways are not our ways.

Somewhere along my way to Biloxi, I ran over something, which made my trailer tire look like it had run over the rod at my house. The only difference was that my tire was still inflated, not even low on air.

The man asked, *"How far did you drive to get here?"*

I replied, *"It took me five hours to get here."*

He looked at me and said, *"You drove all that way with this load on that tire?"* And followed with these words, *"It's a miracle your tire did not blow out!"*

I said *"Yes, it is, and I do Believe in Miracles!"*

I DO NOT believe in coincidences, however, only divine intervention. I'm afraid to think what would have happened if I had not been obedient and bought that new tire. I believe I would have suffered the consequences. Seeing is believing, even if we don't get to see miracles like this every day.

I was so stunned at what I saw that I took a picture of the tire at that moment. I also took a picture of the road to remind me of God's faithfulness and to remind me that God knows my future and what's coming next even when I don't see it. The outcome of this could have ended very differently if I had not been obedient.

CHAPTER 20

The Christmas Miracle

Spring of 2013 was a very lonely time for me. I felt defeated, unhappy, and very alone; my joy was gone, along with my anointing. I felt all dried up inside, and I wasn't seeking God as I had in years past, nor was He using me or talking to me anymore. I cried out and said, *"God, what's wrong with me, and why do I feel this way? God, where are you?"*

What made me so happy all the time was my relationship with God. He was number one in my life. Material things, money, and success weren't important to me. Those things had stopped mattering after I surrendered my life to God years ago. What was important to me was being a servant for God and being used for His glory...

I just wanted back what I had, what filled me up deep inside. I cried out, *"God, please! I don't care what you have to do in my life. I want my anointing back. I want all I had before and more!"*

Was I desperate? Yes! The thought did cross my mind after I pleaded with him that I may not like what He asks me to do, but I didn't care at that point. I felt my life was utterly empty. It had literally no meaning anymore.

I felt as if I was drowning. My body was sinking deeper and deeper underwater. It was as if my head bobbed up and down, struggling for breath as I was pounded by the waves. I could barely gasp for breath as I thinly held on to the hope of survival, reaching my hand up to God and saying, *"PLEASE SAVE ME!"*

When you go through deep waters, I will be with you. When you go through rivers of difficulty, you will not drown. Isaiah 43:2 | NLT

A few months later, I was at the bank when I saw my friend, Raymond, who had recently moved back and was hoping to get a preaching job at a small church in Oak Grove. When our conversation ended, we went our separate ways, and that's when I heard God say, *"Change churches. I want you to start going to the church Raymond will be preaching at."*

I thought to myself, *God, why do you want me to move from my big church to a very small church?*

In the end, as it always seems to be with me, I didn't know why God wanted me to change churches. I just knew I had to be obedient. God's will for me was what I wanted to do with my life, and He was directing me again.

The Lord directs the steps of the godly. He delights in every detail of their lives. Psalms 37:23 | NLT

Our family started attending the small church with about a dozen other members where Pastor Raymond was the new pastor at that time. I didn't know what God was going to do in my life, I just knew He was going to do something. A few months passed, when one morning while grocery shopping, I ran into a customer who used to shop at my store, Just a Touch of Heaven, before I closed down. She stopped me and said, *"I sure do miss your store. Do you think you will ever open it back up?"*

My reply was, *"I miss it, too, but I have no intention of opening the store back up again."* I should have snatched those words back up and eaten them at that very moment, before God made me eat them His way.

I know God has a sense of humor because every time I say NO or say I'm NOT going to do something, He makes me eat those words! There was already a Christian book store in my hometown of Oak Grove, which had opened up about a year earlier. And we surely didn't need two Christian stores in our small town. One of the owners of the other store contacted me when they opened to see if I wanted to rent a spot. I could bring in my own displays and sell my framed poetry, jewelry, and other items I designed, plus my line of inspirational T-shirts. I decided to take them up on their offer so my customers could still buy my items.

The last week of September, I received a phone call from the Christian book store. They had moved their store downtown and left my merchandise and displays at the previous location. The deal we had was changing, and if I moved my merchandise to the new location, I would have to do consignment on all items. I told the owner of the Christian book store I would not be going to the new location. She then indicated that I needed to pick up my displays and merchandise in the next day or two.

This was not a good time for things to be changing, as I had store and internet orders to fill and no place to move everything to. I decided to call the owner of the building, JoAnn, to ask if she had any plans for renting out that location before Christmas and explained that I didn't have anywhere to store my displays. JoAnn graciously replied with, "No, I'm not going to worry about renting it out now because this is my busiest season for my Western store." She agreed to let me store my displays in the building until after Christmas so I would have some time to look for a place to permanently store them.

That wasn't God's plan, however. The next week, God told me to open the store for Christmas. I could get my sister,

Cindy, to work the store while I continued doing my shows and online and wholesale orders. I didn't really want to open a store again. However, some of my displays and merchandise were already there. It wouldn't take me but a couple weeks to have everything ready to open for the Christmas holidays. The question still lingered in the back of my mind, though, *was this really God's will?*

I had mixed emotions because the other Christian book store was in Oak Grove. Plus, I would be moving into their previous location. What if their customers got confused? I figured that I could do this since it was only for a couple of months and through Christmastime. I could order extra things for the store to sell. However, I still wasn't 100% sure. I wouldn't have to do much at all to move in, and the cost would be minimal.

I still wasn't convinced, but it wouldn't hurt to inquire, right?

I needed to call JoAnn to ask about the rent, plus I would have a light bill to pay. JoAnn had purchased the old Walmart building and made six stores out of it, like a mini-mall. I had no idea what I would be paying in electricity. I did not want to rent it and then find out my electric bill would be in the thousand-dollar range. I knew if this was God's will for me, everything would fall into place.

The first piece fell into place when I called JoAnn to see how much the rent would be for October, November, and

December. I told her not to get any ideas because I would only be there till Christmas, that was it! She said, *"I'll take $250 a month. That's what you paid for the small spot when you were renting from the Christian book store."*

Wow! I thought. *A whole store for that price—this must be a God thing!* However, I told her I had to call the electric company to find out the average amount my bill would be before committing. Again, under a hundred dollars a month with a deposit of only $150. At this point, I was totally convinced this was God!

Why would God want me to open a second Christian store in our small town, though? Should I walk through the door God just opened for me or not? I was trying to come up with a good explanation as to why God would do this, reminding myself that His will is what I wanted in my life and that this could be an answer to my cry for God's help months earlier.

The last thing I had to do was call my sister, Cindy, and ask her if she wanted to work for me at the store. She said, *"Yes!"* I was now three for three, and I knew it was God.

On that very day, I paid JoAnn for the three months of rent, picked up the keys, and my oldest daughter, Nicole, and my sister, Cindy, and I went to the store to take a look. I was sitting on the counter when I saw a vision of a little girl's piece of white furniture against one of the walls in the store. I looked at them both and told them the vision I saw. I asked them if they had anything like that I could borrow.

Both replied that they didn't, and they didn't know where I could find anything like that either.

On that same day, after Nicole and Cindy left, I stayed at the store to pray and seek God. I went to the front door, standing there looking out toward the other door that was the entrance to the building where my first store was located. It was only forty feet away, and I remembered all the signs, wonders, and miracles God had accomplished while I was there.

Tears streamed down my cheeks, as I knew all that God had done there. How was this store going to measure up? I then said to God, *"It's not going to be the same."* I no longer had my big waterfall because I sold it a few years after I closed the first store. And the most important thing to me was that I no longer had my cross.

With a yearning heart, I said to God, *"Do you remember that cross, the miracle cross you had me give away? Do you know how important that cross was to me? You took my miracle and gave it to someone else! I wanted that cross in my home, and you knew that, but you still had me give it away!"*

By this point, I was crying so hard because God had opened the door to another store, and I did not have my cross. I try always to be obedient to God. Even though I did not want to give my cross away, I knew I had to. Even though it was a miracle to me, it was a material thing, and I knew I couldn't hold on to it no matter how important it was.

I then heard God say, "Leisa, that was a different season. This is a new season.

I will give you new miracles."

For everything, there is a season, a time for every activity under heaven. Ecclesiastes 3:1 | NLT

The next day came, and I had forgotten all about the vision God gave me the day before. I was at the store with Pastor Raymond who was also a carpenter, along with his wife, Sister Dixie. I hired Pastor Raymond to do the few things that needed to be done before I moved in.

We were there about fifteen minutes when I felt the urge to go check my email.

I walked over to the counter where my phone was laying, opened up the app for my email, and suddenly a Facebook post popped up. My first thought was, *How did that happen?* When I looked at the post to see what it was, I couldn't believe what I was seeing! It was the little girl's piece of white furniture I saw in my vision the day before. I jumped up and down with joy, and then the thought crossed my mind, *Oh no, what if they no longer have this anymore? I will be crushed.*

I immediately called the phone number listed in the advertisement. They still had the piece of furniture, and it was mine if I wanted it. I asked where they were located, and I was shocked to learn that they lived just a few miles down the road from me. Wow! That was a God thing for sure!

Everything went as scheduled, and I had the grand opening the last week of October. Sales were not what I thought they would be, nor what they needed to be. I was comparing this store with my first store.

One day, JoAnn was at the store when I said something about my sales not being like the first store. She looked at me with a stern voice and said, *"Leisa, forget about that first store. That's in the past. You can't go back there!"* It was like she had slapped me in the face, and I realized at that moment she was right. It was clear to me this store was not going to be like my first store, and I needed to stop comparing them to each other.

On December 7, a Saturday, I was at the store, standing at the counter having a conversation with God and wondering what the heck happened? Did I not get this right? Where were all my customers? Where was everyone? It was a slow Saturday with no customers and only two more Saturdays of shopping remained before Christmas.

I said to God, " *I know I didn't get this wrong, but why am I having these doubts now? You gave me visions and they came to pass, and I'm getting these feelings that you want me to stay here next year. I have to have sales to stay open and pay my bills. This was not what I wanted or asked for! What is going on?"*

I continued, *"God, I need a sign if you want me to stay here because if not, I need to put all my merchandise on sale now. I need to know ASAP!"* I thought about that for a few minutes and said, *"God, I need a Miracle Sign for me to stay here. I need to know without a shadow of a doubt what I need to do. Should I stay or go?"* We had revival coming up from December 8 to December 11, and I was sure hoping God would send me a sign at that time.

Sunday morning, Canaan and I went to church while Gary was off working. Evangelist McGee was preaching that morning, and the service was coming to a close when I heard the Evangelist say, *"I see a waterfall!"* Oh, my gosh!

That got my attention quick. A waterfall was the first thing God told me to buy for the store before I opened up years ago. He went on to say, *"There's someone here who used to be anointed just like a flowing waterfall. But now you're just a trickle. Don't tell me you're the reason I had to travel all the way from North Carolina to say this. God said you can have it back if you want it, and more!"*

Did I just hear what I thought I heard? Oh, Yes! I wanted to jump up and down with joy because I knew he was talking to me. No one knew I had cried out to God except God and me. That's it. I never told anyone what I was going through. I had cried out to God months prior, asking for my anointing back, and God sent the Evangelist to a small church in Oak Grove just to tell me that.

I realized if I had not been obedient when God told me to move to that church, I would have missed the message that

God wanted me to hear. God can't make us be obedient; it's our choice. That's why it's so important for me to be obedient to God, because maybe there is someone waiting for a sign, answer, or miracle from God, and I'm the person God will use to help them.

This time it was me who was looking for the sign, an answer, a miracle. Hearing that message that morning renewed my Faith, and I felt as though I was soaring on the wings of an eagle.

But those who trust in the Lord will find new strength. They will soar high on wings like eagles. They will run and not grow weary. They will walk and not faint. Isaiah 40:31 | NLT

Monday night at the revival, God told me to give the Evangelist $500 as an offering. This was not Tithing; this was an extra blessing for the Evangelist.

I pulled out my business checkbook to see what my balance was, and I had a little over five hundred dollars. God knew that was my money to pay my bills with. I thought, *God, I'm struggling here with the store, and you want me to give five hundred dollars?* I knew it was God, and once again it was clear. He wanted to know how much I trusted Him.

Trust in the Lord with all your heart; do not depend on your own understanding. Seek His will in all you do, and He will show you which path to take. Proverbs 3:5-6 | NLT

The next Tuesday morning, I got a call from Pastor Raymond who said, *"We need a cross for the Wednesday night service. Can we borrow yours?"* Well, the first thing I thought was that cross was too big for them to be able to use it. I told him I no longer had that cross. God had me give it away years ago. He asked, *"Who has it? Do you think they would let us borrow the cross?"* My mind flooded with many thoughts, *Pastor you are a carpenter, you could make a cross. The cross is in a glass case. It's not going anywhere.*

Pastor Raymond was determined to get the contact information for the man I had given the cross to. I told him I couldn't remember his name and I didn't know how to get in touch with him, but I finally said, *"Pastor, I will see what I can do to find him."*

I felt stupid. However, the thought of maybe getting to see my cross again put a spark in my heart. I hung up the phone and started searching. I could only remember a small portion of the name of his store, and his flower shop was located in Jena, Louisiana. I searched the internet and finally found his business and the phone number. His name was also listed on the website as well. It was Lavelle.

As I was sitting on my couch thinking about the day Lavelle came to pick up the waterfall, which was five feet tall and five feet wide. I remember looking at the trailer he brought and laughing as I said, *"Are you sure you have a long enough trailer?"* It was about twelve feet long. When God told me to give Lavelle the cross that day, I understood why the trailer was so long—because the cross was ten feet in length. God always comes prepared.

I was crying as I gathered up the robe and the crown of thorns, thinking I would never see my cross again. Lavelle said to me, *"Are you sure you want to do this?"*

My reply was, *"Yes, I'm sure!"* I felt like my heart was breaking into a million pieces (not understanding why God would do this to me).

Lavelle told me he knew how special the cross was to me, and he promised he would take good care of it. He had big plans for the cross, and he was going to put a glass case over it because he knew the story and thought the cross was something special.

I sat there with my phone in my hand thinking, *Oh, God, maybe I can see the cross again, just one more time.* I prayed, *Oh, God, please let this phone number be correct and Lavelle still be in business.* I picked up my phone and called. No answer, but a recording came on. I was excited because that meant he was still there. I then heard God say, *"Leisa, call from your cell phone."*

I picked up my cell phone and called back. Lavelle answered. I said, *"Hello, Lavelle,"* and told him who I was since it had been years since we talked. We had been talking for about fifteen minutes when I told him I had opened my store again. I paused and heard nothing for about ten seconds. Then I heard, *"Leisa, would you like to have your cross back for your store?"* Are you kidding me!? I was so excited, I could hardly believe what just happened.

I said to Lavelle, *"YES! Thank you."*

Lavelle answered, *"Leisa, I guess God wanted me to be the keeper of the cross for a few years."*

I told Lavelle I would get someone to come pick it up, and I hung up the phone and called my husband, Gary, immediately to tell him what had happened. When he answered his phone, I went into the whole story about Pastor Raymond calling me and wanting to borrow my cross I no longer had. I knew this was the miracle sign I asked for from God. I continued asking Gary if he believed this was a sign from God?

His reply was, *"I don't know."*

I said, *"Why don't you know?"* I was really getting frustrated with his answers.

I heard him say, *"Leisa, Pastor Raymond did not need your cross!"*

Now I was really confused, *"What do you mean Pastor Raymond did not need my cross? Yes, he did. He called me this morning."*

Gary said, *"Leisa, I called the Pastor this morning asking for a favor. I asked him to call you and find out who you gave the cross to so I could call them to see if they would let me buy the cross. I wanted to give it to you as a Christmas present!"*

I sat there stunned, thinking about everything that just happened. I couldn't stop crying, my tears flowing like Niagara Falls. My first thought was how much my husband must love me, but then I realized how much God must really love me too! Today God was saying NEVER lose your HOPE!

For I know the plans I have for you, says the Lord.
They are plans for good and not for disaster,
to give you a future and a hope. In those days
when you pray, I will listen. If you look for Me
wholeheartedly, you will find Me.
Jeremiah 29:11-13 | NLT

Yes, this cross was my miracle, but the true miracle of the CROSS was when

God sent His Son, Jesus, to die on the cross for us so that we might live. It's our choice.

The message of the cross is foolish to those who
are headed for destruction! But we who are being

saved know it is the very power of God.
1 Corinthians 1:18 | NLT

God is all-powerful, and He uses people as stepping stones to get us each to the next step. He will open doors no man can close. Even though it was never my prayer that I would get my cross back, He truly knows the desires of our hearts.

Take delight in the Lord, and He will give you your heart's desires. Commit everything you do to the Lord. Trust Him, and He will help you.
Psalms 37:4-5 | NLT

CHAPTER 21

The Invitation

Do you feel empty inside? Have you been searching for something out there, and you're just not sure what it is? Well, there's a man I know, and His name is JESUS!

He is LOVE...

For God so loved the world, that he gave his only begotten Son, that whosoever believeth in him should not perish, but have everlasting life. John 3:16 | NLT

His name is greater than any other name!

Wherefore God also hath highly exalted him, and given him a name which is above every name: that at the name of Jesus every knee should bow, of things in heaven, and things in earth, and things under the earth; And that every tongue should confess that Jesus Christ is Lord, to the glory of God the Father. Philippians 2:9-11 | NLT

He is the great I AM...

I AM the Bread of Life...John 6:35

I AM the Light of the World...John 8:12

I AM the Good Shepherd...John 10:11

I AM the Resurrection and the Life...John 11:25

I AM the Way and the Truth and the Life... John 14:6

I AM the True Vine...John 15:1

I AM Alpha and Omega, the beginning and the end, the first and the last... Revelation 22:13

He said you'd be forgiven of all your sins.

If we confess our sins, he is faithful and just to forgive us our sins, and to cleanse us from all unrighteousness. 1 John 1:9 | NLT

He can deliver you from drugs, alcohol, or any other addictions.

No more emptiness or loneliness inside. He can set you free of all things.

There hath no temptation taken you but such as is common to man: but God is faithful, who will not suffer you to be tempted above that ye are able; but will with the temptation also make a way to escape, that ye may be able to bear it. 1 Corinthians 10:13 | NLT

If the Son, therefore, shall make you free, ye shall be free indeed. John 8:36 | NLT

For he hath said, I will never leave thee, nor forsake thee. Hebrews 13:5 | NLT

I am with you always, even unto the end of the world. Matthew 28:20 | NLT

You are worthy, and you can be a child of the MOST HIGH GOD!

....they shall walk with me in white: for they are worthy. Revelation 3:4 | NLT

If you don't know JESUS as your Lord and Saviour just ask Him to come into your heart now!
Therefore if any man be in Christ, he is a new creature: old things are passed away; behold, all things become new. 2 Corinthians 5:17 | NLT

Behold, thou art made whole: sin no more, John 5:14 | NLT

JESUS said: I say unto you, there is joy in the presence of the angels of God over one sinner that repenteth. Luke 15:10 | NLT

Your name is in the Lamb's Book of Life and you will spend eternity in Heaven with Him.

I will not blot out his name out of the book of life, but I will confess his name before my Father, and before his angels. Revelation 3:5 | NLT

May the Lord Bless You and Keep You and His Peace Be with You Always—

Leisa, *"A Servant for the Lord"*

Epilogue

After what happened in the story *"The Christmas Miracle,"* my husband came home for Christmas from his job. He traveled four hours to pick up my cross and bring it back to the store. Pastor Raymond put it up for me. That same day I thought about hanging a burlap sculpture bust of Jesus on the cross I had ordered while I was at my first store years ago.

I climbed up the ladder and placed it above the beautiful robe. I then climbed back down, walked away about fifteen feet, and turned around to see what it looked like. It was breathtaking! Pastor Raymond agreed it needed to stay there.

A few days passed after hanging up the cross when I heard God say, *"Take a picture of the cross from the floor up."* I thought that was a great idea as I already had one from my first store, and I would have a picture of this store to save along with it.

As I was standing there thinking, I wondered why God would want a picture from that angle. The other picture I had was a straightforward shot from the front. I went to my office and got my chair, and set it down about six feet from the cross. I couldn't see how I was going to do it. After about five minutes of squirming around in the chair trying to take a good picture, nothing seemed to work. That's when God said, *"Leisa, flip the camera on the phone and hold your arms down to take the picture."*

I did what God told me to do, taking the picture in that manner. My hair on the back of my neck stood straight up! I then heard God say, *"Leisa, that's the picture for your book, add these words, "I LOVE YOU THIS MUCH. — JESUS."*

What a moment—I stood there looking at my book cover! The picture had to be edited to remove the wall so it would have a black background, but other than that, it was complete.

In the last month, God gave me the ending to my book, *"The Christmas Miracle"* story, and the cover for the book. It was now complete.

However, I knew it would be all in God's timing, as to when I would send the book out to the world.

Wait patiently for the Lord. Psalms 27:14 | NLT

A few months later, God told me to buy a mannequin, and buy all the items needed to look like a Roman Soldier. My first thought was, *God, I don't think I can find a mannequin that could pull that off.* However, if He was telling me to do this, there had to be one out there that would work.

After days of searching, I found it! This mannequin was standing at attention with his hands behind his back, just like what a soldier would do. I ordered it. Then I had to find all the gear, clothing, and shoes, replicas of the Roman body armor, and helmet.

I thought I would be able to find the Halloween Roman outfit made of plastic. However, what God had waiting was not made of plastic like a Halloween costume. I found everything I needed to complete this soldier to look like he was a Roman Soldier, I was amazed! The body armor and helmet was made of steel and shipped from India. I received everything, dressed him up, and I put him standing right beside the cross.

Even though I did everything that God told me to do, the store could barely pay its bills. In August of 2014, God said, *"Close the store after Christmas."* This devastated me! I loved praying for people and telling my stories of all the signs, miracles, and wonders God had done in my life. I knew I didn't get this wrong. I knew this was God's will, but why open and spend so much money, going into debt only to close fourteen months later. I just couldn't comprehend why.

However, in the month of December, God showed five people just how miraculous He can be.

The first week in December, I was at the house when I heard God say, *"Leisa, I want you to give away your SUV."* For a second, my thought was, *Is there anything else you want to take from me?* Yes, I was still upset over the idea of closing the store and being in debt. Now He wanted me to give away my SUV!

Even though I didn't want it to be God telling me this, I knew it was. I said, *"God, who am I supposed to give it to?"*

God said, *"Give it to the church."*

I then said, *"When am I supposed to do this?"*

God's only reply was, *"You'll know."*

I said, *"God, will you please let me get moved out of the store first? I will not have a way to go anywhere!"* My husband didn't have a vehicle. He only had a company truck, and he was always off working. Our son, Canaan, had a truck, but have you ever tried borrowing a teenager's vehicle? Ha!

Now, how was I going to tell Gary that God told me to give away my SUV? A few days before Christmas, Gary and I were both at home. We were sitting in the living room when I decided I needed to tell him. I said, *"I need to talk to you about something."*

"What is it?" he asked.

I said, *"God told me to give away my SUV."*

He looked at me with a mean look, and in a stern voice said, *"If you think you are going to give away your SUV and I'm going to go buy you another vehicle, you are sadly mistaken!"*

I sat there in total shock. For him to think I was doing this as a trick so he would go buy me another vehicle was very upsetting. After all the stories—the signs, miracles, and wonders God had brought forth in my life, and he says this to me!? I'm sure I had a look of sheer disbelief on my face.

He continued, *"Who are you supposed to give it away to?"*

My reply, *"The Church."*

"When are you supposed to give it away?" he asked.

I said, *"I have no idea. God just said I would know when it's time."*

After Gary didn't believe God told me to give away my SUV and accused me of scheming to get a new vehicle, I started praying. I needed God to reveal to him that it was He who told me to give away my SUV and not a scheme on my part.

Christmas came and the sales at the store were low. I was hoping for a miracle because in my heart I didn't want to close.

After Christmas, I had everything in the store, except for my t-shirts, marked 50 percent off on the first day and then 75 percent off the second day. Everything was going as planned. However, I had some t-shirts I wasn't going to have printed anymore and thought this would be a good time to mark them down to $2.50 to get rid of them. I would work at the store the next day, pulling T-shirts from the back, putting them on the shelves by size and style, and hanging some on the racks as well.

I was on my way to the store to start pulling T-shirts out when I heard God say, *"Leisa, I want you to get off of Facebook."*

My reply was, *"But God, that's how I advertise the T-shirts and the jewelry I make. If I don't have Facebook, how will people know about my sale tomorrow?"*

God replied, *"So you have more faith in Facebook than you have in me?"*

"Oh, no!" I cried. When I got to the store, I deactivated my Facebook page.

I called JoAnn, the owner of the building, to tell her about the sale I was going to have the next day and that after that time, I would be permanently closed. She came over after she closed her store that evening and picked out six or seven t-shirts.

The next morning, I called my sister, Cindy, and told her to let her friends know I was having this big sale on my t-shirts. I also called Sharon, the owner of a beauty shop, and told her to please tell the customers who came into the beauty shop that day.

When I drove up to the store that morning, there was already a line waiting outside the door. I unlocked the door and let them all in. I hopped on the register, and Lisa (my best friend) and her mom, Jean, bagged up the t-shirts as shoppers checked out.

I was on the register nonstop for about an hour. Most of the people were buying ten to twenty t-shirts each. I looked up expecting to see half of the T-shirts gone, but all I saw were the shelves disheveled.

I mentioned it to Lisa and she looked and said, *"That's weird because we have bagged up so many for sure."*

People were still pouring in as I wondered where they were coming from. I continued to check out nonstop and decided to stay open until 4:00 p.m. It was crazy how many people showed up for the sale, leaving with arms full of merchandise.

Around 3:00 p.m., I looked up again, stunned by what I saw. It looked just as it had hours earlier! *How was this POSSIBLE?* I thought to myself.

I said to Lisa, *"Do you see what I see?"*

She said, *"Yes, I do! You are selling hundreds of t-shirts, and it doesn't look like you've sold that many. The shelves still look full!"* Lisa continued, *"How is this possible?"*

I said, *"I'm glad I'm not the only one who sees this."*

Jean said, *"We are even out of bags. People were buying bags full!"*

At that moment, I heard, *"Leisa, if I can take two fish and five loaves of bread and feed over five thousand, I can replenish your t-shirts so you can make more money."* All of our minds were blown!

Jesus took the five loaves and two fish, looked up toward heaven, and blessed them. Then, breaking the loaves into pieces, He gave the bread to the disciples, who distributed it to the people. They all ate as much as they wanted, and afterward, the disciples picked up twelve baskets of leftovers. About 5,000 men were fed that day, in addition to all the women and children.
Matthew 14:19-21 | NLT

I ran the reading on the register, and I was shocked! It showed my sales were a few dollars short of $1,700.00. How was this possible? At $2.50 each, I would have to sell over six hundred and seventy-five shirts to reach that amount. I didn't even have that many shirts for sale. I counted what was left and stopped counting at 250.

I then called JoAnn and said, *"JoAnn, you were here last night. How much do you think I would make if I sold all the t-shirts I had for sale?"*

She replied, *"Oh, probably five or six hundred dollars."*

I told JoAnn what I had made and she said, *"No way! Not at $2.50 each. Maybe at your normal price of $16.99."*

I then decided to make a video of the t-shirt display to send to Connie. We had left at the same time the night before so Connie knew how many we had to sell. I asked her to tell me how much she thought I sold. She texted me back and said, *"Oh, no! I was hoping you would sell a lot of your t-shirts, but it doesn't look like you've sold very many."*

I replied, *"How much do you think I made?"*

She replied, *"By the look of it, not too much, maybe two to three hundred dollars."*

I replied, *"Connie, my sales were a few dollars short of seventeen hundred."*

"THAT'S IMPOSSIBLE!" she replied. *"You didn't have that many tees out there to make that much money, especially at $2.50 each!"*

WOW! All five of us saw the miracle that day, and I'm convinced if I had not trusted God and exited Facebook, we would not have seen that miracle at all.

The following Sunday morning, Gary, Canaan, and I were at church, and the sermon Pastor Raymond was preaching on was—trust the Lord with all your heart, even when you don't understand it! The sermon was closing when the pastor said, *"Sister Dixie and I started praying for something about a month ago, and we are both believing God will answer our prayers."*

He continued to say, *"I have to make four or five trips every Sunday morning to pick people up and bring them to church because they don't have a way to go and we only have a truck. Sometimes having to make so many trips causes me to be late for church, and we need a bigger vehicle."*

In that moment, I was sitting there thinking, *Yes! Thank you, God!* My SUV was extended and held eight people. I turned to look at Gary, and the look on his face was as if he had just seen a ghost! I said, *"It's time!"*

After the service, we both went to the pastor and told him God had told me about a month ago that I was to give the church my SUV. The pastor was stunned with the way it happened. Gary was leaving, going back off to work the next morning, and I was very thankful that God revealed to him that it wasn't a scam for me to get a new vehicle. He really did tell me to give my SUV away to the church. I had all the paperwork complete a few days later and handed the keys over to the pastor.

Even though my heart was broken when I closed the store, I knew I had to open the store in order for God to give me back my cross and reveal to me the cover and the ending to my book.

It was God's purpose for me to open the store, but not to stay there. My dream is that one day God will build me my prayer room so I can have my cross and soldier displayed there to remind me that NOTHING IS IMPOSSIBLE WITH GOD!

Special Thanks

First, thank you, God, for never giving up on me, and giving me this purpose to share with the world. Thank you for all the miraculous signs, miracles, and wonders you performed in my life. Thank you for sending Your son, Jesus, who sacrificed His life for me so I would have everlasting life with Him in Heaven.

Second, to my parents, Nancy and Jerry. Thank you for loving me and giving me life. I asked God eighteen years ago to please allow you both to live long enough so you could see His Glory through me. You are both still here after each battling cancer. His Glory is here and you both will see. I Love You!

Third, to my husband, Gary, my children, Nicole, Chelsi, and Canaan. Thank you for your love and for believing in me. I hope all my stories of Faith and Trusting God has helped all of you to grow and believe that with God all things are possible. I Love You!

Fourth, to all my family and friends who stood beside me and believed in me.

You know who you are. I Love You!

And fifth, to my editor, Rachel. Thank you for all your hard work. I could not have written this book any earlier. I don't believe I would have found you earlier. You were a Godsend for sure. I know I was probably an unusual client with the demands I had about not changing my words. May the Lord bless you abundantly!

About the Author

Leisa Spann believes in faith, miracles, signs, and wonders. She has experienced them all. It is through these experiences that she testifies of God's goodness and mercy and shares that goodness with others.

Leisa has worked in retail for more than 20 years and currently designs and makes handcrafted jewelry, framed poetry, and other Christian-based gifts. She tells people that her boss is Jesus, and she loves working for Him! She enjoys writing poetry, staying involved in her community, and serving in her church.

Leisa lives in Oak Grove, Louisiana with her husband, Gary. She has three children, Nicole, Chelsi, and Canaan, and four beautiful grandchildren who she hopes will grow in their own faith and know that with God, all things are possible.

Website: LEISASPANN.COM

Email: leisaspann@yahoo.com

Made in the USA
Monee, IL
16 March 2021